"What?!? We had homework??"

Email Reminders to Clients from DBT Skills Class
Leaders

Kristin B. Webb, PsyD

Permission to use "Seven Steps of Participating" on p. 103, Meggan Moorhead, EdD with Mareah Steketee, PhD. Used by permission (personal communication, April 8, 2020).

Permission to use material on pages 104-106 from Marsha Linehan, <u>Skills Training Manual for Treating Borderline Personality Disorder</u>, 1993, pp. 123-124. Reprinted with permission of Guilford Press.

Permission to use "42 Ways to Say No", on pp. 107-108, © Margot Silk Forrest, "A Short Course in Kindness". Used by permission (personal communication, February 21, 2020).

Permission to use material on pp. 109-110 from Seth Axelrod, PhD, adapted from Marsha Linehan's <u>Skills Training Manual for Treating Borderline Personality Disorder</u> (1993). Used by permission (personal communication, February 19, 2020).

Permission to use VITALS on p. 112 © Meggan Moorhead, Norma Safransky, & Bill Wilkerson. Used by permission (personal communication, April 9, 2020).

Permission to use materials on pp. 115-116, Mareah Steketee, PhD., and Chuck Holton, LCSW. Used by permission (personal communication, April 2, 2020).

Permission to use "Holiday Antidotes" on pp. 117-118, John Mader, LCSW. Used by permission (personal communication, February 20, 2020).

Printed by Kindle Direct Publishing in the United States of America.

First printing edition 2020.

Kristin B. Webb, PsyD
104 So. Estes Drive, Suite 206
Chapel Hill, NC   27514

www.drkristiwebb.com

Dr. Kristi Webb received a Master's in Counseling Psychology (M.A.) and a Doctorate in Clinical Psychology (Psy.D.) from Antioch University New England. She is a Licensed Psychologist in North Carolina with over 20 years' experience in a variety of treatment settings, including inpatient psychiatry, psychiatric emergency services, community mental health, substance abuse treatment, eating disorders day treatment, and a Veterans' Administration hospital. She taught psychology for several years in Vermont, New Hampshire, and North Carolina. Since 2001, she has been in private practice, where her focus is individual therapy with adults. Her primary area of expertise is Borderline Personality Disorder; as a result, she also treats depression, anxiety, and trauma and its sequelae, including substance abuse, dissociation, and self-harming behaviors. Dr. Webb is an intensively-trained Dialectical Behavior Therapy (DBT) therapist as well as an Archetypal Pattern Analyst. She is a member of the North Carolina Psychology Association, and was active for many years on its Colleague Assistance Committee. She can be found at www.drkristiwebb.com, Facebook.com/DrKristiWebb, and YouTube.com/DrKristiWebb.

I am always so grateful for my DBT skills class co-leader, Jennifer Kern Pennell. Working together since 2005, we have seen the lives of countless emotionally sensitive people transformed by DBT skills. On the acceptance-change continuum, she is Acceptance and I am Change. We make a great team.

I am an individual DBT therapist and have been co-leading DBT Skills Groups since 1999. My co-leader and I have found that clients/patients are more likely to practice the skills and do their weekly homework if they receive emailed reminders three to four days after the class meets. These are also useful to those who were absent from class. This volume contains all of the reminders I send out weekly.

I send these reminders to each group member and their individual therapist. I blind copy all recipients so that their email addresses are not disclosed. All page numbers in the reminders refer to Marsha Linehan's DBT Skills Training Handouts and Worksheets, 2nd edition.

Of course, the prompts might be useful following an individual session as well. You are free to use any of these reminders – or all of them – as long as you give credit to Dr. Kristi Webb, Chapel Hill, NC. You are free to edit them, with the same caveat – please give credit for the original reminder to Dr. Kristi Webb, Chapel Hill, NC. In fact, since it takes us an entire year to cover all the skills, if you are on a tighter schedule, you will need to combine some of these prompts, which you are welcome to do as long as you give credit.

When using email, of course, HIPAA security questions arise. One way to manage this is to use secure email (examples include Hushmail, G Suite, or SendInc, among others). Another option is to describe your DBT skills class as just that: an educational class, rather than a therapeutic one.

Purchasers of this book who wish to copy and paste from it into emails for their skills class members can access a Word document (.doc) version of the book at htttps://www.drkristiwebb.com/my_book. The password you will need for access to the page is wVRyMZhw – this will allow you to download the document for your professional use.

Thank you for your interest in this collection of DBT skills reminders.

CONTENTS

Skills Reminders for the Core Mindfulness Module

Dear DBT skills class,

This week we are learning about what kinds of problems bring people to DBT - maybe you saw yourself in the list of behaviors to decrease, or in the biosocial theory.

On General Handout #1 (p. 9) we named specific behaviors to decrease by using DBT. These include a sense of internal emptiness; judgmentalism; interpersonal conflict; difficulty regulating your emotions when you want to; an inability to ride out crises without hurting yourself or someone else, or without making the situation worse; and impulsive behaviors. You might take the handout with you to your next individual therapy appointment so that you can identify what skills you especially want to learn, or what behaviors you want to decrease, through this class.

On Handout #4 (p. 13) is a list of the assumptions that DBT therapists and skills trainers make about folks who come to us. Some of these assumptions are: people are doing the best they can; they need to do better, try harder, and be motivated to change (just because you're miserable doesn't mean that you're doing enough to solve the problem); all behaviors are caused; and that figuring out what caused the behavior - and changing it - is more effective than blaming.

Handout #5 (pp. 14-15) is a quick-and-dirty lesson on the biosocial theory that underpins all of DBT. In brief, the theory says this: emotional dysregulation is the result of biological factors (some people are born with emotional sensitivity and they are more prone to impulsivity than others) plus an invalidating environment (one that ignores your emotions or tells you that they're wrong), plus the interaction of biology and the environment over time. We spent some time describing characteristics of an invalidating environment in more detail. For example, there is an intolerance of the expression of emotions and emotional experiencing. Specific emotions are labeled "weird", "bad", or just plain "wrong." The message conveyed is that you should be able to handle emotions without support. Problem-solving is presented as very easy ("just do X"). Finally, the invalidating environment ignores emotional reactions, leading you (the emotionally sensitive person) to escalate in order to get your needs met.

The homework for this week is General Handout #1a on page 10. Usually, our homework is found in the worksheets, so this week is a little different. Use the handout (homework) to examine in detail one specific situation you encounter this week - or one that recurs that you struggle with. Decide which of the options you want to use with this problem, and if you already know some of the skills, try them - can't wait to hear what you come up with!

Wishing you a good and mindful week.

DBT Reminder: States of Mind

Dear DBT skills class,

This week we are diving into the Core Mindfulness module. We started by examining why we bother to teach mindfulness. What does it have to do with reducing your emotional sensitivity? Research shows that a practice of mindfulness reduces rumination, anger, irritability, and chronic pain; it increases one's ability to cope with physical and emotional pain; it improves physical health. Who doesn't want to suffer less and be happier? Mindfulness lets you increase your control of your own mind - what you pay attention to and for how long. Avoiding what bothers us never teaches us to cope with it; mindfulness helps us gently approach, not avoid.

Many people come to DBT thinking that mindfulness is relaxation and that if they don't "feel better" or "feel calmer" after practicing mindfulness, they didn't get it. Mindfulness is simply <u>deliberately paying attention</u>. Instead of going through our day on autopilot, we live with awareness in the present moment. It is really, really hard! There are numerous apps to help you get started, such as Insight Timer or Headspace.

One of the Core Mindfulness skills is Wise Mind, and in order to understand Wise Mind we must first understand Emotion Mind and Reason (or Rational) Mind. Here in the Triangle area of NC we also refer to Body Mind (you won't find this in your skills manual, though).

<u>States of Mind</u>

Emotion mind - contains all our emotions; is hot, spontaneous, and often impulsive; and is useful when we are looking to laugh or be passionate. Having strong emotions is not the same as being in EM, though; we're in EM when our emotions are running the show, when they're in control.

Reason mind - contains our analytical part, and is particularly useful when we will benefit from rational thought, logic, and cool problem solving. Think about following a recipe or balancing your checkbook.

Body mind - holds all of our physiological responses and feelings; it is often useful to tap into this part to identify how we are doing, and what we may need (such as rest, food, softness). It is also useful to look to Body Mind for clues about our emotions because they may first manifest as somatic experiences (tightness, stomach pain, clenched fists, fatigue).

Wise mind - a balanced place, where we can achieve a calm sense of knowing. WM includes information from EM, RM, and BM, so a Wise Mind decision takes all the other states of mind into account. Often, when we make a decision from a place of Wise Mind, we experience relief. Everybody's got a Wise Mind.

The Handouts we studied this week are 1, 1a, 2, 3, and 3a in the CM module (pp. 45-52). The homework is CM Worksheet #3 (p. 83).We look forward to hearing about your experience with this!

DBT Reminder: "What" Skills of CM

Dear DBT skills class,

Last week we learned about the states of mind - Reason Mind, Body Mind, Emotion Mind, and Wise Mind. This week we launched ourselves on the path to studying specific mindfulness skills, using Core Mindfulness Handout #4 (p. 53). These skills help us to take hold of our mind, instead of our minds controlling us.

So, <u>what</u> do we do, in order to get into WM? Three skills: first, we talked about the skill of **Observe**. Observing is simply noticing, without judgment or evaluation. We do this during the Mindfulness practice at the start of each DBT class. You notice what you are experiencing through your senses. We can observe objects, events, and our own thoughts or feelings. We cannot observe other people's thoughts, motives, emotions, or intentions. We can observe with a narrow focus (for example, watching what our mind does when we count to 10, or we notice our bellies rising and falling with each breath) or with a wide focus (notice your thoughts; notice your body sensations). We can observe inside us or outside of us.

We then added the skill of **Describe**: to put words on what we are experiencing. Once you've observed your thought, feeling, or body sensation, put it into words. This skill lets us tell the difference between what we observe and what we don't observe (because you can't describe something you haven't observed). It helps us to regulate emotions.

Finally, **Participate** by getting into the flow - of your thoughts or feelings or body sensations, of this one moment, of your breath, of an activity. Attached to this you will find the Seven Steps of Participating we talked about in class.

Everybody will likely have difficulty with one of these three skills. Some people struggle to observe without analyzing, thinking, and ruminating, as if the skill of Describe is in overdrive; others do nothing but Observe, staying on the sidelines of life and not Participating (this is most likely to be true if you're socially anxious). Some people are able to Participate, but they do it in a way that drives other folks crazy, and because they aren't using the skill of Observe, they don't notice.

We urge you to try this over the next week. The homework is CM <u>Handouts</u> 4, 4a - 4c (pp. 54-59) and <u>Worksheet</u> 4 <u>or</u> 4a <u>or</u> 4b (pp. 84-87). You'll find many, many suggestions on the handouts of how to practice these skills; the worksheets offer a variety of ways to log your practice. At least three times, try one Observe suggestion, one Describe, and one Participate. We look forward to hearing what you try.

This may all be very confusing at first. You are learning a new language as well as a new way of looking at yourself and the world. Don't give up! Bring your questions to your individual DBT therapist and to class and we'll do our best to answer them.

Dear DBT skills class,

Once we know <u>what</u> to do to get into WM, we can turn our attention to <u>how</u> to do it. We're on CM Handout #5, page 60.

When we are **Nonjudgmental**, we are only thinking and talking about the facts. "I feel bad" means nothing; "I feel sad, angry, hurt, and discouraged" is non-judgmental (just the facts). "I shouldn't have eaten that piece of pizza" is judgmental; "I wish I hadn't eaten that piece of pizza" captures the facts of the situation without judging. Judgmental words that we avoid include (but are not limited to) *bad, good, should(n't), ought(n't), always,* and *never*. It's true that there are situations in which discernment or evaluation is necessary; teachers, for example, compare students' answers on a test to a standard. That's not what we're talking about; we're talking about letting go of judgments that are our opinions. We practice this skill because being judgmental, by definition, means we're in EM; because judgments can damage relationships; and because judging something doesn't change its cause - it doesn't solve the problem.

Being **One-Mindful** is similar to Participating: this skill asks us to concentrate only on one thing at a time, in the present moment. Our culture promotes the myth that multi-tasking is efficient; it is not. Research shows that multi-taskers tend to make more mistakes and then have to go back and ask questions or repair their error. Using this skill will decrease your physical, mental, and emotional misery.

Being **Effective** is focusing on what works rather than on what should work, or what you wish would work. In order to be effective, you must first know what your goal is. The skill necessitates some Radical Acceptance (another skill, from the Distress Tolerance module) of things as they really are rather than as we wish they were, or as they ought to be. We deal with the reality of what <u>is</u>, and that's effective. Being effective often requires letting go of words like "unfair" in favor of your goal. Do you ever scream at the automated voice prompts on the phone - not very effective, is it?

The homework for this week is to use CM Handouts 5a, 5b, and 5c (pp. 61-63) in order to complete CM Worksheet 5 <u>or</u> 5a <u>or</u> 5b <u>or</u> 5c on pages 88-93 .

DBT Reminder: Other Perspectives on Mindfulness

Dear DBT skills class,

In addition to the specific skills we have been learning (<u>what</u> to do to get into Wise Mind; <u>how</u> to do it), we are also taking a look at some other ways to use mindfulness in our daily lives. Mindfulness is used for spiritual, psychological, medical, and/or humanistic reasons.

As we have already learned, mindfulness is about experiencing reality as it actually is (rather than as we wish it were). This will require a "spacious mind", which is the opposite of rigidity and inflexibility. When we are highly emotionally aroused our minds tend to become constricted and inflexible. That is, when we're upset we tend to respond in the same old way we always have. DBT is teaching you a flexible repertoire of responses.

Mindfulness helps us grow in wisdom -- another way of saying that mindfulness helps get us to Wise Mind (WM). We become balanced: heart <u>and</u> brain. It's very practical. It helps us experience freedom: we can want something we can't have and nonetheless have a life worth living - even without it. We can be free of the despair that keeps us longing for something we can't have.

We also want to increase love and compassion for ourselves and for others, and mindfulness helps us achieve this. We can increase our sense of connection to others by practicing loving kindness through mindfulness. When life gets hard, it's really easy to feel isolated, alone, and unconnected; this can be extremely painful. All of us feel disconnected at some times, but the ongoing sense of no connection to others often arises from a belief that the world must go the way we want it to go if we're going to feel happy. It can also come from having a very rigid idea of what connection looks like. Mindfulness helps us build a feeling of connection and overcome loneliness.

CM Handouts 7 and 7a on pages 68-69 provide a variety of spiritual perspectives on Wise Mind. The existence of Wise Mind is a universal belief (although obviously it is not always called that). This handout offers a variety of ways to think and talk about it.

CM Handout 8 (page 70) is about loving kindness and practicing it in order to increase our love and compassion for ourselves and others. Loving kindness might be defined as mentally sending warm wishes. Ill will toward others is exhausting and - research shows - physically harmful to ourselves (and sometimes to others). Practicing loving kindness reduces self-hatred, increases our interpersonal effectiveness, and increases positive emotions. It fits well with other skills, such as GIVE (in IPE), OTEA (in ER) for anger and disgust toward others or yourself, and Imagery (in DT). This handout includes instructions for practice, which you will do for the homework.

The homework is CM Worksheet #6 on page 97. We look forward to hearing your adventures with this.

DBT Reminder: Balancing Doing Mind and Being Mind

Dear DBT skills class,

This week we studied Core Mindfulness Handout #9, on page 71. The idea is that in our daily lives, being in Wise Mind requires us to balance our drive to achieve goals (Doing Mind) with experiencing whatever comes next for us (Being Mind). The tension between these two states of mind is similar to that between Reason Mind and Emotion Mind. This week's material may be especially helpful to those of us who are overachievers, driven to accomplish.

Doing Mind is relentlessly task-focused. It's all about ambition. We need Doing Mind in order to cross items off a list, to plan, to get work done, to meet goals. Too little Doing Mind and we won't achieve goals that are important to us. Too much, however, and we become Type A people, workaholics, perfectionists. Some people will use artificial means (caffeine, certain drugs) to keep themselves in Doing Mind.

But in Doing Mind we lose sight of the value of the present moment - we're always looking to the past or to the future and evaluating how close we are to or far we are from some future goal. In **Being Mind**, we are open to and curious about the moment we're in. Think of being with a child: that child continually invites you to play, to be in Being Mind, to have nothing else to do and nowhere else to go but be right there with the child. It's also possible to have too much Being Mind - we can be so focused on our own experiences that we seem narcissistic and self-centered, or irresponsible and self-indulgent. Of course, there are times when we must be in Doing Mind, in order to plan or to follow a map, or to respond to emails. As in all of DBT, the key is balance.

The homework is to use Handout #9a (lots of practice suggestions, pp. 72-73) to complete Core Mindfulness Worksheets 7, or 7a, or 8, or 9 on pages 98-104 (your choice of formats; also, 7a, 8 and 9 emphasize Being Mind over Doing Mind). On Worksheet #7 the goal is to get into Wise Mind; it's not about relaxing or calming down or feeling better.

We look forward to hearing your experiences balancing Doing Mind and Being Mind.

DBT Reminder: Walking the Middle Path

Dear DBT skills class,

This week we talked about walking the middle path, or finding the synthesis between opposites. You may remember that the definition of "dialectical" (as in Dialectical Behavior Therapy) is "the tension between two opposites". Two things that seem contradictory are both true at the same time. Generally speaking, when we are at an extreme on any continuum, we are in danger of distorting reality. The goal of all of the DBT skills is to help you find the balance point, or the middle path, between all and nothing, good and bad, red light and green light, Emotion Mind and Reason Mind. We studied Core Mindfulness Handout #10 on page 74.

As we know, Wise Mind is found at the intersection of Emotion Mind and Reason (or Rational) Mind. In WM, we replace either-or thinking with both-and thinking. In WM, we make decisions that take into account both thoughts and feelings, both facts and strong emotions. When we try to synthesize Doing Mind and Being Mind, we walk the middle path of doing just what is needed in this moment, although we also take into account our past experience and our plans for the future. We may have a very strong desire that things be different right now and a willingness to radically accept things just as they are - that's the middle path. For example, passionately throwing yourself into achieving your goals while at the same time being willing not to quite get there, is the middle path. When we choose to buy the small popcorn at the movies we are choosing the middle path between self-indulgence (the super-giant large size <u>and</u> a soda) and self-denial (nothing at all).

Balance isn't always a 50-50 split. Also, what's balanced for one person may not be balanced for the next person. How do <u>you</u> know you're on the middle path? What is "out of balance" for you?

We also talked a bit about dialectical abstinence, which is used with addicts and alcoholics (and we define addiction as being to more than just drugs; it could be food, gambling, spending…). Dialectical abstinence is the balanced point between complete abstinence and complete relapse; it's sometimes called harm reduction.

The homework is found on CM Worksheets 10, 10a, and 10b on pages 105-108. You can choose to do just one or all three. Worksheet 10a offers you step-by-step instructions to practice finding the middle path, the point of balance between two opposites.

Dear DBT skills class,

This week we completed our study of the skills in the Core Mindfulness module. Mindfulness isn't relaxation; it teaches us to approach the uncomfortable emotions and experiences, rather than doing whatever it takes (which sometimes gets us into trouble) to avoid them. The purpose of being mindful is to experience reality just as it is; to increase your control of your mind; and to reduce your own suffering and increase your happiness. Who wouldn't want that?

DBT emphasizes balance. Wise Mind is a balance between Reason Mind and Emotion Mind. Wise Mind is also a balance between Doing Mind and Being Mind: both are necessary.

We asked <u>what</u> to do to get into Wise Mind: we use the skills of Observe, Describe, Participate. You observe your experience to see what is, to take in information. Describing your experience means putting it into words, as you would if you were telling another person. But thoughts are not facts, and the skill of Participating helps us make conscious, aware, intentional choices about our actions (rather than being reactive). Participation without awareness is a key characteristic of impulsive and mood-dependent behaviors.

We also learned <u>how</u> to get into Wise Mind: Nonjudgmentally, One Mindfully, and Effectively. When we are Nonjudgmental, we are only thinking and talking about the facts; we're in Rational (or Reason) Mind and staying out of Emotion Mind. Being One-mindful asks us to concentrate only on the here-and-now; we don't have to add the suffering of the past or the future to the present moment. Being Effective is doing what works, using skillful means. In order to do this, we must know what our goal is and then we can choose thoughts and behaviors that are consistent with our goal.

The homework for this week is to use CM Worksheets 2, 2a, 2b, and 2c for your review of the CM skills. They are on pages 78 - 82. Remember that this is a practice, and is meant to help you play around with these ideas and concepts to see if you are able to experience them first hand. It is <u>not</u> about being perfect at any of the CM skills. Keep in mind that (like all of the DBT skills), they become easier (less hard) with practice. Try to use them deliberately when you do not need them, such as during a mundane moment.

Wishing you a good, mindful week.

Skills Reminders for the Core Mindfulness 2-week review

(used between modules)

Dear DBT skills class,

We are reviewing the Core Mindfulness skills, so that we're all on the same page starting out. Each of the CM skills helps foster self-awareness and deliberate focus on the present moment, which are fundamental building blocks for increasing your control over your experience.

We started by getting familiar with the States of Mind (p. 50 in the manual). These are **Body Mind** (what your body is sensing at the moment); **Emotion Mind** (just your feelings, no thoughts, no logic); **Reason Mind** (all logic and reason, no feelings, like Mr. Spock from Star Trek); and Wise Mind (where the other three intersect). We then looked at What To Do to get into Wise Mind. (This coming week we'll look at How To Do It).

The first skills involve taking a step back from your immediate experience and just noticing it. **Observing** does this without words, and **Describing**, with words. Stepping back itself can be very helpful and is a necessary part of gaining greater control over your experience and behavior. These are also helpful skills when things feel overwhelming or distressing, and you need some distance to take stock of the situation.

If, for example, you are worrying about something, you can observe to yourself that you are experiencing worry thoughts, visualize them floating away or off the end of a waterfall (observe) or label your thoughts as "thoughts" or "worries" (describe). You can also observe and describe anything outside of yourself. Try to keep your descriptions short, simple, and nonjudgmental.

Participating is quite different -- rather than observing your experience, the idea is to engage fully in it. Try to participate as you do a puzzle, engage in a challenging work situation, make or listen to music, savor a chocolate, create something, take a walk, or any other activity in which you can lose yourself (even if only for a moment.) You can also participate in an emotion and, odd as it may sound, you can practice this with uncomfortable emotions too. If you are in a situation in which you can devote yourself to the emotion, try to focus all of your attention to it. Experience it. Notice how it feels. Paradoxically, when we do this, the emotion tends to shrink and turn up with less intensity later. We've attached the Seven Steps of Participating.

The goal of practicing these three skills is to increase our ability to participate in life with awareness.

For homework this week, complete the worksheet on States of Mind. You may "catch yourself" in the moment or deliberately set out to Observe, Describe, or Participate - and then write down what you notice. What does Body Mind say? What does Emotion Mind say? What does Reason Mind say? And what does Wise Mind say? We look forward to hearing how this went for you.

Wishing you each a good, mindful week.

Dear DBT skills class,

This week we are finishing our introduction to the Core Mindfulness Skills. We learned the "how to" (be mindful) skills of Nonjudgmentally, One-mindfully, and Effectively.

The skill of **Non-judgmentally** invites you to stop labelling things as "good" or "bad" and instead to describe observable facts and consequences. Judgments take us immediately into Emotion Mind. Discernments are a necessary part of life: think of grades or a judge's sentencing. Judgment, however, assigns labels: good/bad, smart/dumb, fat/thin. When you observe a judgment, try to substitute a more neutral description by sticking to "just the facts" or describing consequences. A clue that you're judging is hearing yourself use certain buzzwords, such as good, bad, awful, must, should, always, never, can't. For example: If you find yourself saying, "I'll never feel better," or "What a terrible person," break your judgment down to the relevant facts, such as, "I don't have as much energy as I had hoped to, by now" or, "I find how he behaves distressing and I wish he wouldn't behave that way." Keep in mind that most people make judgments (both favorable and unfavorable) very frequently. Becoming aware of your judgmental thoughts helps to deflate their power. This is a difficult skill that requires practice (and often a new way of thinking and self-talk). There are lots of practice suggestions in the Core Mindfulness module's handouts 5 a - c. As you practice this skill, do not judge your judging!

Acting **One-mindfully** helps you to stay in the moment and to direct your attention to whatever is immediately at hand. Practice paying attention to your food when you are eating, the interaction when in conversation, or to your breath when walking or meditating. The aim is to be present with your immediate experience, whatever it is. Yes, you can plan ahead - but do so one-mindfully, being completely present to your planning. Multitasking is inefficient, and the pain of this moment is enough for anyone (without adding the pain of yesterday, or the pain you might feel in an hour, to it). Conscious effort is required for this skill. Eventually, as you practice this and it comes more easily, you will be able to approach, not avoid, your uncomfortable or afflictive feelings, observing them non-judgmentally and dealing with them effectively. Which brings us to…

Practicing **Effectively** requires that you identify your goal in any given situation and then follow through with thoughts and behavior that are consistent with this goal. While this may sound easy, the potential for derailing from this course is great, such as focusing on what is fair/unfair, or what we think "should" (a judgmental word) be happening, or having feelings of self-righteousness or indignation. Being effective often requires letting go of these in favor of your goal. Have you ever screamed at the automated voice prompts on the phone - not very effective, is it?

The homework assignment is: please complete CM Worksheet 5, 5a, 5b, or 5c on pages 88 - 93. We suggest choosing <u>either</u> 5, 5a, or 5b (one of those three - they cover all of the skills, just in different formats), <u>or</u> 5c, which focuses only on non-judgment.

Use the inevitable challenges that arise during this week as opportunities to experiment with these skills. Next week, we will embark on the _________ module.

Skills Reminders for the Interpersonal Effectiveness Module

Dear DBT skills class,

This week we began our study of the Interpersonal Effectiveness (IPE) module of skills. We looked at IPE Handouts 1, 2, and 2a, starting on page 117. Our goal in this module is to teach you to do three things (these are on Handout 1):

1. Ask for what you want or say "no" and be taken seriously;
2. Build healthy relationships and end destructive ones.
3. Walk the middle path of balance between acceptance/change and between your needs/others' demands.

Achieving interpersonal goals is hard work; that's why there are lots of skills in this module. There is also no guarantee of success - sometimes, no matter how skillful you are, the environment is just too powerful. It's not you. We also talked about how our skill level will vary depending upon the situation: some of us are quite skillful at work but not with our families; most of us are not skillful when we're tired or hungry.

Handout 2 talks about factors that can get in the way of being interpersonally effective. These can include:

1. Lacking skills (but we're going to remedy this!);
2. Not knowing what you want (you can't decide, or have conflicting goals, or you don't know how to walk the middle path of balance);
3. Your emotions get in the way (usually anger, fear, or shame);
4. You give up your long-term goals in favor of a short-term goal; that is, you go for the gusto right now instead of hanging on for something better later (sometimes your short-term goal is to decrease your distress);
5. Environmental factors that are outside of your control, e.g., how others may respond - no matter how skillful we are, sometimes we won't get what we want. Sometimes the environment is just too powerful; and/or
6. Your myths (thoughts, beliefs) about interpersonal situations get in your way

That last factor that gets in the way led us to Handout #2a, Myths in the Way of Interpersonal Effectiveness. We all (even your leaders!) have some worries about standing up for ourselves, asking for help, expressing opinions, or saying "no" to others. Some of these worries are based on myths about interpersonal behavior that we picked up in our early years and some are learned through later interactions that didn't turn out as well as we'd hoped.

The homework is going to be IPE Worksheet #2 (pages 168-169), which asks you to try to counter your myths. It is very important that your challenge be one that you will buy into; don't try to take the position 180 degrees different from your myth. If you believe, "My needs have to come after everyone else's" you're probably not going to believe that "my needs have to come before everyone else's." But you might believe that "Sometimes my needs have to come before everyone else's except my children's." Attached you will find a handout that is from the first edition of the DBT Manual. It has cheerleading statements for IPE that can be used to challenge your interpersonal myths.

We look forward to hearing everyone's stories.

Dear DBT skills class,

This week we covered Interpersonal Effectiveness Handouts #3 and #4 on pp. 123 and 124, and talked about the importance of knowing what our goals are before we launch ourselves into any interpersonal interaction. In every interpersonal interaction, three things are at play: getting what we want (our objective), keeping or improving the relationship, and maintaining our self-respect. We'll have to pay attention to <u>all three</u> of these things in every interpersonal interaction, but the emphasis will change, depending upon our priorities:

1. We want to have **objective effectiveness** - This refers to your goal in the situation, what you are looking to achieve. After the interpersonal interaction (the conversation, phone call, meeting), what do you want to be different?

2. We want to have **relationship effectiveness** - This focuses on acting in such a way as to maintain or improve a relationship <u>even if you don't get what you want</u> in the interaction.

3. We want to have **self-respect effectiveness** - This focuses on how you want to feel about yourself after the interpersonal interaction <u>even if you don't get what you want</u>.

It can be a real challenge to discern exactly what your goal is in a specific situation. Usually, figuring out what we want to have be different when the interaction is over (our goal, or **objective effectiveness** as DBT calls it) is pretty straightforward. "I want you to listen to me." "I want my money back." "I want to change my appointment time." "I want you to pick up your room." But let's say, for example, that you have been looking forward to having some down time to do some things that you value, and someone asks a favor of you. Your objective would be to preserve your down time. **Relationship effectiveness** has to do with how you want the other person to feel after the interaction (based on your handling of the interaction), with having the other person continue to like you, with balancing your short-term goal (have down time) with the long-term health of the relationship. Your relationship effectiveness goal might be, "I want my friend to understand that I need some time off right now," or "I want my friend to feel that she can count on me whenever she needs me." As for self-respect, you will want to act in a way that is consistent with your values and beliefs and that would preserve your self-respect, such as being honest, gentle and kind. Your **self-respect effectiveness** goal could be, "I want to express my limits without shouting" or "I want to feel proud of myself that I problem-solved and negotiated so we could both get what we wanted."

For homework this week, complete IPE worksheet #3. It's on p. 173. Use your skill of Describe to say what the prompting event is, that created the problem to be solved. Then bring your examples to class.

Wishing you each a good, mindful week.

Dear DBT skills class,

This week, we introduced the "DEAR MAN" skill (IPE Handouts 5 and 5a on pages 125-127). DEAR MAN is the "script" of what you are going to say in your interpersonal interaction, regardless of which goal is your priority.

There are 3 goals that are present in all interpersonal interactions: Your **objective**, your **relationship** goal, and your **self-respect** goal. DEAR MAN is emphasized when the **objective** (making a request, resolving a conflict, getting your rights respected, getting your opinion taken seriously, saying no and making it stick) is your top priority.

In the conversation, here is how to use DEAR MAN:

1. **Describe** - state the facts, and only the facts, non-judgmentally. Strive for 25 words or less.

2. **Express** - your feelings or opinion, avoiding "you should," "you always," "you need to," etc.

3. **Assert** - ask for what you want or say "no". Do this very clearly so that there is no room for misunderstandings. Assertion is not the same thing as aggression!

4. **Reinforce** - include an incentive that increases the other person's willingness to help you or to be able to tolerate you saying "no" without feeling rejected. This could be your appreciation, or some other way that they will also benefit. The other kind of reinforcer is when you tell the other person what will happen if you don't get what you are asking for. For instance, "If I don't get a raise, I'll have to start looking for another job." "If you don't ask permission before using my car, I will call the police and report it stolen next time." Remember, if you specify a consequence ("I will start looking for another job"), you must be willing to follow through.

Throughout the conversation,

5. Stay **Mindful** - Keep your focus on your <u>goal</u> in the situation, maintain your position, and don't be distracted onto another topic. Two helpful techniques for staying mindful:

a. <u>Broken Record</u>: Keep asking, saying "no" or expressing your opinion over and over and over. Go back to the top of your script and just keep saying the exact same thing.

b. <u>Ignore</u>: If the other person attacks, threatens or tries to change the subject, ignore it. Repeat your point. The other person's responses are a big, fat, juicy worm; don't take the bait!

6. **Appear** confident - Use a confident tone of voice and physical manner with appropriate eye contact. No stammering, whispering, or staring at the floor.

7. Be open to **Negotiate** - Be willing to give to get. It can be helpful to go into any interpersonal situation knowing how much you are willing to give up, in order to get what you want. Knowing your priorities helps answer that question.

For homework, Worksheet #4 on page 174 gives you practice writing a DEAR MAN script. Your leaders rarely go into an interpersonal interaction without a DEAR MAN GIVE FAST script at least in our heads; sometimes we still write it down and read it out loud to the other person, if we are in danger of falling into EM. You may also want to look at Handout 5a on page 127, which gives an example of what this sounds like in a difficult interpersonal interaction.

We look forward to hearing your DEAR MAN scripts. Bring successes as well as ones that have you stuck that you want help with. See you in class!

Dear DBT skills class,

This week we reviewed the GIVE skill, on IPE Handouts 6 and 6a, pp. 128-129. This skill is about improving or maintaining a relationship, while simultaneously trying to get your objective met. This is always used in conjunction with DEAR MAN and FAST. Remember that we really emphasize GIVE when the relationship goal is our #1 priority. So it's always there, but sometimes it's a little "louder."

GIVE stands for….
(be) **Gentle**, that is, nice and respectful
(act) **Interested**, which we love because it doesn't say you have to <u>be</u> interested, just act it.
Validate the other person's point of view (this is useful at any time, not only when you're in the midst of a conflict)
(use an) **Easy** manner, and humor is very effective

Some additional hints to make this go more smoothly:
1. Be aware of your body language when you're trying to be gentle. Remember that humans believe non-verbal signals before we believe words.
2. One can "act interested" simply by listening and keeping eye contact. You don't have to become engrossed or fascinated; not interrupting or talking over the other person is sufficient!
3. Handout 6a goes into more detail about how to validate. The most basic approach is simply to pay attention; do this in every interpersonal interaction. Validation is an effective skill to use when trying to improve or maintain a relationship.

The homework is IPE Worksheet #5 on page 175. We can't wait to hear more examples of your IPE practice in class.

Wishing you all a good and mindful week!

DBT Reminder: FAST

Dear DBT skills class,

This week we introduced the interpersonal effectiveness skill FAST (IPE Handout #7 on page 130). We will include FAST in every interpersonal interaction because maintaining our <u>self-respect</u> is essential. Sometimes you'll make it your #1 priority. When you don't stick up for yourself, you can end up feeling taken advantage of and resentful; on the other hand, never giving in can make you seem harsh and abrasive, and that also decreases your self-respect. This skill means we are **Fair**, without **Apologizing**, **Sticking** to our values, and being **Truthful**.

F: To give yourself the courage to ask for what you want or to say " no", practice talking to yourself the way you would counsel or support a friend. For example: "It makes sense that I feel frustrated/sad/anxious/angry right now." "I bet this is hard for most people." "It's okay that this is scary right now." Balance fairness to yourself with being **fair** to the other person. Consider the other person's emotions and wishes, too. It is hard to respect yourself if you are always taking advantage of others or if you are always putting your wants and needs behind others'.

A: If you tend to over-**apologize**, practice avoiding the words "I'm sorry" (except when it is appropriate because you did something against your values and want to express remorse). Watch out for apologizing for having an opinion, for having a point of view, or for disagreeing with another. Watch out for the "I'm sorry to ask..." sort of apologies and for words like "just" and "little", as in "I'm just asking for a little favor…" This minimizes your needs and wants. Apologizing when it is not called for can have negative consequences on self-respect.

S: **Stick** to your values unless the consequences will be dire and life-threatening. If you are not sure whether that is the case, borrow someone else's Wise Mind.

T: Being **truthful** refers to avoiding repeated, habitual dishonesty. "I didn't get your email" or "I definitely returned your call - didn't you get it?" are examples of dishonesty that erodes our self-respect, over time. We also avoid acting helpless; if you can solve a problem, and you act in ways that communicate that you don't know how to, that's being helpless. You can practice being both fair and truthful by saying what is on your mind (rather than stomping around frustrated, exaggerating your grievance for effect, or at the other extreme pretending something did not bother you when it did).

Remember that the IPE skills (DEAR MAN GIVE FAST) aren't just for our intimate relationships and are not just for crises. Attached are two pages of suggestions for situations in which you can practice your skills. Look for opportunities to practice on the mundane things of daily life as well as with more serious matters that come up in your personal life. As with the other skills, the more you practice them, the more natural and comfortable they will feel. In those cases in which you would like to try FAST but it feels too difficult to try (as in breaking patterns with family members), try your hand at writing out what you <u>would</u> say in ideal circumstances.

The homework is, again, IPE Worksheet #5 on page 175. If you can't identify an interpersonal interaction that took place this week to write about, use one from the past and report on what you would have done if you'd had this skill; or use the homework to plan for an upcoming interaction in which self-respect is your #1 priority.

Dear DBT skills class,

This week we learned what factors to consider so that you can increase or decrease the intensity of your work to change things (by saying "no" to a request, or by asking for what you want). It can be difficult to stand up for yourself, and sometimes we may be unsure if it is "our right" or even "in our best interest." IPE Handout #8 on pages 131-133 presented 10 factors, or conditions, that you can consider to determine how intensely to ask or to say "no." The "Options" box on page 131 lists varying levels of intensity; you may find the descriptions useful.

The factors to consider (page 132, with descriptions of each on pages 132 and 133) are sometimes rather basic (can this person even give you what you want? Is this person required by law to give you what you want?) and at other times will require more thought on your part (how will your asking or saying "no" affect your self-respect? what's the degree of give and take in this relationship? have you done your homework before asking or saying "no"?).

In #3, Self-Respect, we don't care for Linehan's use of the phrase "feel bad about yourself"; we encourage you to consider whether saying "no" to a request will violate your Wise Mind values, leave you feeling incompetent, or cause you to lose respect for yourself. Just because we feel guilty about saying "no" doesn't mean it was the wrong thing to do - it might be that emotional myths are producing the guilt, rather than a lack of self-respect.

The homework is to use Worksheet 6 (The Dime Game) on pages 176-177 to tally up these factors to help you with decision-making about the intensity your request merits. This exercise is to help figure out the extent to which it makes sense to try to tolerate things as they are versus doing something to try to change them. Try to match your word choice to the intensity of your desire for change. For example, if you score a 9/10 on the worksheet, this represents a strong desire for change, thus insist and try to "make it stick" rather than backing down. If you find your desire is more like a 1 or 2/10, then you might raise the issue without insisting (again, we prefer not to "hint indirectly").

In our experience, the hardest thing about this skill is deciphering the handout. Most of us have a bit of an instinct about some of the factors to consider. For example, if you have kids or co-workers, you know how you react when they catch you with a request just as you're coming in the door, before you've even taken your coat off (if you're like me, you react poorly). This is the factor of timing (#10). On the handout, it may help to remember that the factors are written so as to apply to <u>both</u> asking for what you want <u>and</u> saying no.

Have a skillful week.

P.S. We have also attached a handout, "42 Ways to Say No" - we think you'll find it useful.

DBT Reminder: Troubleshooting IPE Skills

Dear DBT skills class,

      This week we are studying IPE Handout #9 on pages 134-135, which addresses what steps to take if your IPE skills aren't working. The accompanying worksheet (for homework) is IPE Worksheet #7 on pages 178-179, which is probably a bit easier to use than the handout, in a situation where your skills didn't work the way you had hoped or expected them to.

      The handout provides a checklist for when your Interpersonal Effectiveness skills "don't work". The list is in a specific order, from most likely to least likely:

      1. Do you know what skills you need? Do you know how to use each of them? Have you followed instructions to the letter, not skimping anywhere?

      2. Have you clarified your goals (objective, relationship, self-respect) and your priorities?

      3. Are short-term goals (like being right, or venting) getting in the way of long-term goals (like acting out of Wise Mind)?

      4. Are emotions getting in the way of using skills? Are your emotions so high that you're past the point of being able to access the IPE skills and need to turn to Distress Tolerance?

      5. Are worries, myths, and/or assumptions getting in the way of using skills? Are you telling yourself stories such as, "She'll get mad if I say no" or, "I can't do this"?

      6. Is the environment just too powerful? Sometimes, no matter how skillful we are, we're just not going to get what we want.

      The homework is Worksheet #7, pages 178-179. It is so very important to practice these skills, so please do! It's perfectly appropriate to do the homework using some interpersonal situation from your past that went horribly wrong.

      Wishing you a skillful, mindful week.

Dear DBT skills class,

Last class we moved into a new section of the Interpersonal Effectiveness module, which deals with building relationships and ending destructive ones. IPE Handout 10 (p. 139) gave us an overview of what we'll be covering over the next few weeks, namely finding and getting people to like you, building closeness through mindfulness of others, and ending destructive or unhealthy relationships.

We spent most of our time on IPE Handout 11 (p. 140-141), Finding and Getting People to Like You. We started with the assertion that all human beings are lovable (by someone, even if not by you). This means that you, too, are lovable. It doesn't mean that people are going to flock to you just because you've been through DBT, though, so you're going to have to use some skills in order to have people in your life that you enjoy doing things with.

So what factors are important in finding and making friends? First is <u>proximity</u> (people who are nearby). This means that places like your gym, church, or a class you're taking are great places to meet people who might become friends. It's important to say, "Yes!" when someone invites you to join a group or a project or to go for coffee. Next is <u>similarity</u>; this is the basis for Meetup groups, that bring together folks who like cats, or French films, or who are single parents. Similarity is a double-edged sword, though, because some similarities can make others feel uncomfortable. This is why it's not wise to disclose your personal problems very early in forming new relationships. Next up is a recommendation that you <u>work on your conversational skills</u>. Never underestimate the value of chit chat. Have a list of stuff that you can talk about (besides the weather), like a movie you've recently seen, or March Madness, or the news headlines. "You show me yours and I'll show you mine" is a useful rule, here: you don't want to undershare - you do want to disclose something personal in order to increase closeness with a potential new friend - but you don't want to overshare, either. Don't interrupt, and plan that your contribution to the conversation will be about 50%. The next factor is to <u>express liking selectively</u>. This doesn't mean sucking up, but people like people who like them, so if you offer praise to someone it's likely they will feel good about you. It can be effective to express liking of someone's characteristics selectively, to notice and appreciate something unusual about the person. Asking questions of the other person can be very flattering. When accepting compliments, practice saying, "Thank you!" and then shutting up. Our last factor this week was <u>joining a group</u> to meet people. We need to have two important skills in order to do this: knowing if a group is open or closed; and figuring out how to join an open group conversation. We can also join an organized group, like a team or a choir. It's more effective if these groups meet often, have people in it who are similar to you, and are larger rather than smaller. Groups that cooperate, rather than compete (Habitat rather than a tennis team) are more likely to produce friendships, research has shown.

The homework for this week is on two pages: <u>Handout</u> 11a (we call this the Cosmo Quiz), which is on page 142, and <u>Worksheet</u> 8, which is on page 183. Bring us your disasters (we love those and have some of our own!); bring us your thrilling successes. We look forward to hearing about your efforts to find and get people to like you.

Dear DBT skills class:

This week we turned to how to <u>promote, maintain, and improve relationships</u>. We turned to IPE Handout 12 (page 143) to talk about being mindful of others: "Friendships last longer when we are mindful." You already have these skills, yay! They are Observe, Describe, and Participate.

Observe by paying attention, being interested and curious, being one-mindful (no multitasking when with the other person), being non-judgmental, and focusing on the other person. Be open to new information about someone (not to do so is invalidating). Stay away from being rigid. Give up being right; you can have friends or you can be right, but not both. Don't respond to anxiety either with isolation or with an over-focus on yourself (as in, talking only about yourself).

Describe by putting words on what you see, rather than making interpretations. Instead of saying, "you're mad at me", try saying, "I noticed that you gave me only a short answer to my question and that you weren't meeting my eyes. Is there something going on I should know about?" Here, you've used the Describe skill instead of being judgmental, assuming, or interpreting. It can be useful to use a matter-of-fact approach, the who-what-when-where kind of description, or just the evidence of your five senses. Stay away from assumptions, jumping to conclusions, and remember that consequences are not the same as intentions. Give people the opportunity to earn your trust; having too little trust and too much trust are both problems. Give others the benefit of the doubt. Stay away from a hyper-focus on your own performance; it keeps you from being present to what actually is going on.

Finally, use the skill of **Participate**: throw yourself into interactions with others. Go with the flow, rather than trying to control it. This is hard to do if you're anxious. You may need to use additional skills such as One-thing-in-the-moment and Opposite to the Emotion Action.

The homework for this week is Worksheet #9 on page 184. The top part should be fairly straightforward, as it is a checklist. The bottom part requires that you write a bit of narrative about what happened. We challenge everyone to be sure to complete your homework, at least the top half. You can certainly report on what you *would* do if you *were* interacting with someone - even if you don't interact with anyone, or you didn't practice.

"Trust but verify" ~Ronald Reagan

DBT Reminder: How to End Relationships

Dear DBT skills class,

This week our topic is how to end relationships; we studied IPE Handouts #13 and 13a. These refer not only to romantic relationships, but to friendships, jobs, and even some family relationships, at times. Especially if the relationship is <u>destructive</u> or <u>interfering</u>, these are the skills to use.

A <u>destructive</u> relationship is one that destroys or spoils something: your physical safety, self-esteem, happiness, peace of mind, or the relationship itself. These are the relationships that are called "toxic."

An <u>interfering</u> relationship blocks your ability to achieve your goals, or decreases your ability to enjoy life, or interferes with the welfare of yourself or those you love.

If a relationship is neither destructive nor interfering, you might consider the pros and cons of ending it. Take the long-term view; you might stay in the relationship if the cost of leaving is greater than the cost of staying. Use the skill of problem-solving (from the Emotion Regulation module) to figure out if there is a realistic hope for improvement in the relationship. You will likely have to get others involved (for example, your therapist) in figuring this out.

The first rule of ending relationships is, "safety first". The second rule is, "never end a relationship when you are in Emotion Mind!" But if you do choose to end it, you already have the skills to do so. You may already have used Pros and Cons (from Distress Tolerance) and Problem-solving (from Emotion Regulation); next use Cope Ahead (from Emotion Regulation) to practice how you're going to end things. Write a script ahead of time and practice it out loud. Where will you be? What time of day will it be? What if you get push-back? Use your IPE skills (DEAR MAN GIVE FAST) to be direct, to validate the other person's perspective, and to be fair to both of you.

Even if the relationship is destructive or interfering you may have trouble ending it. Here is where you can use the skill of Opposite to the Emotion Action (OTEA) which is from the Emotion Regulation module. OTEA for love means avoiding the person and reminders of them, distracting yourself from thoughts of and feelings about the person, stopping expressing your love, and reminding yourself why you have to end things.

The homework is Worksheet #10, page 185. Make it up, if you have to: use an imaginary friend or job, or a celebrity, or apply it to a previous relationship (whether you ended it or not).

Wishing everyone a mindful week with healthy relationships.

DBT Reminder: Dialectics

Dear DBT skills class,

Last class we used IPE Handouts 14, 15, 16, and 16a-c (pages 149-154). Handout 14 gave us the overview of this portion of the IPE module, which is all about moving away from extremes. We'll be teaching several ways to manage yourself and your relationships, starting with Dialectics, which is where we spent the rest of our time.

Dialectics is the tension between two opposites, balancing two things that are both true at the same time, such as good/bad, yes/no, true/untrue, rainy/sunny. There are four guiding principles:

1. There is always more than one way to see a situation and more than one way to solve a problem;

2. Everyone and everything is connected (we influence others <u>and</u> they influence us);

3. Change is the only constant; and

4. Change is transactional, meaning that if you change then your environment must change, which will force you to change again, and so on. Our behavior affects others, and theirs affects us.

Emotionally sensitive people often have a hard time being dialectical. They prefer to establish their position and hold to it, come what may. This seems safer, more secure, less uncertain and wobbly. Emotionally sensitive people tend to engage in all-or-nothing thinking rather than both/and thinking.

Thinking and acting dialectically means asking your Wise Mind, "What's missing in this discussion/situation/argument?" It means letting go of extremes, of the poles, of all-or-nothing thinking. Handout 16 suggests practicing getting used to change by changing small things such as deliberately changing where you sit, what route you take to/from work, or the order in which you get ready for bed. Acting dialectically means paying attention to the effect your behavior has on other people, not only how their behavior affects you. It means identifying with others, not comparing yourself to them. It means validating the other person's point of view even when you strongly disagree with it. I can be right that it's too cold in the room <u>and</u> you can be right that it's too hot.

Handout 16a lists some examples of opposites that can both be true at the same time. We also looked at the list on Handout 16b of important opposites we all must practice balancing. Handout 16c is another (as we call them) "Cosmo quiz".

For homework, please look at Worksheets 11, 11a, and 11b (pages 189-191). We think you'll have the most fun with 11b, which invites you to describe a couple of situations in which you were NOT acting or thinking dialectically; Worksheet 11 is the opposite. That is, Worksheet 11 asks you to describe a couple of situations in which you acted and thought dialectically, and how you did that. Worksheet 11a is a checklist format for your everyday dialectical practice; just check off the exercises each time you try one.

Wishing you a week filled with dialectics and much practice.

Dear DBT skills class,

 In the last class we talked about validating others (IPE Handouts 17, 18, and 18a, pp. 155-157). Validation means finding the kernel of truth in another person's perspective, words, or behavior. It doesn't mean we have to agree ("we come at this from different sides"), but that we can see why the other person would think/feel/act that way. Practicing validation means that we understand that all behavior makes sense in some way - maybe not to us, but to the person engaging in it. It might not make sense given the facts of <u>this</u> situation, but maybe it will make sense when we understand the other person's history.

 Validation is key to building and maintaining healthy relationships. It is essential for building relationships of trust and intimacy. Being invalidated tends to shoot us right into Emotion Mind, which decreases interpersonal effectiveness.

 So how do we do this thing? Handout 18 is a handy-dandy how-to guide. When we validate, we want to communicate our understanding to the other person. We validate a person's experiences, feelings/emotions, beliefs, opinions, or thoughts. The most basic form of validation is paying attention: no multitasking. You can reflect back non-judgmentally, i.e., "I think you are saying... is that right?" Validation can take the form of responding to body language, or what is unstated. We used the example of asking someone for a ride at the end of the day, seeing her shoulders slump, and saying, "You know what? You look really tired; let me figure something else out this time." We also validate by treating the other person as an equal, not as fragile or "too emotional."

 We don't, however, validate what is invalid. So if someone is angry with you for eating the last piece of cake, but you didn't eat it, you might validate that the other person is angry, but you don't validate that you actually ate the cake.

 For homework, we are asking you to complete IPE Worksheet #12 on page 192. Please notice that the instructions say to use the worksheet whenever you <u>do</u> validate another person or when you <u>don't</u> but you could have. Try the Cosmo Quizzes, too; these are handouts #18a and 19a - have fun!

 Wishing you a week of validation.

DBT Reminder: Recovering from Invalidation

Dear DBT skills class,

In class we studied IPE Handout #19, pages 158-159. Recovering from invalidation can be just as important as validating others. Remember that there are several types of invalidation; some are helpful and some are harmful.

Helpful invalidation: This includes corrective feedback that shows you that your facts are wrong, or that your beliefs don't make logical sense in terms of the facts, or that your behavior is not effective for reaching your goals.

Corrosive invalidation: Corrosive invalidation can take many forms. For example, being ignored; not being understood (there is a typo in the skills manual here); being told, "no, you don't feel that way" or the other person giving understandable but incorrect causes for your behavior, or misinterpreting with great certainty your intent for saying/doing something. Any of these make it hard to feel accepted or cared about. Having current facts denied or ignored can have serious consequences, as when you're judged guilty of something you didn't do (such as when your roommate accuses you of eating her yogurt and you didn't). Receiving unequal treatment makes it hard to feel a part of the group.

Traumatic Invalidation: This is extreme or repetitive invalidation of your significant private experiences, characteristics, perceptions, reactions, thoughts, beliefs, emotions, or desires. An example would be telling your mother you were sexually abused and she doesn't believe you. The most extreme example is sexual assault/abuse. Typically, traumatic invalidation comes from a very important person, group, or authority on whom you are dependent for your sense of well-being or personal integrity.

Recovery from Harmful Invalidation: The easiest way to recover is to return to IPE Handout #18 and use all the steps for validating on yourself. Don't try to distract yourself from your distress, but pay attention to what you're feeling; tell yourself it makes sense, given your history and/or what just happened to you, that you'd feel invalidated. Practice radical acceptance of yourself and your feelings - this is especially important if you were invalidated in a helpful way, i.e., you got your facts wrong or you behaved ineffectively. Remind yourself that all behavior is caused (yours and the other person's). Be compassionate toward yourself. Practice self-soothing. Admit that it hurts to be invalidated by others, even if they are right. Remind yourself that invalidation, even when <u>you</u> are right, is rarely a catastrophe. Give yourself room to grieve the harm that traumatic invalidation caused you.

Take a look at IPE Handout 19a on page 160 for some examples of what we talked about. Then complete IPE Worksheet #13 on page 193 as homework.

Wishing you a skillful week.

Dear DBT skills class,

At our last class meeting we studied IPE Handout 20 on page 161, one of three handouts looking at strategies for changing behavior. There are very effective strategies for increasing behaviors that we do want in ourselves or others, and for decreasing behaviors that we don't want in ourselves or others. The secret to effective behavior change is to learn these strategies and put them into action.

To increase the likelihood of desired behaviors we use **reinforcement**: a consequence that increases a behavior. This works on people and animals. Think of the mom in the grocery store line whose kid is clamoring for candy. At first, she ignores him; then she tells him "no!" several times. Finally, exasperated, she gives in and hands him a candy bar. She has just reinforced his behavior: next time he wants candy, he is going to nag and beg and shout, and he can be pretty certain he'll get his candy. Likewise, if every time a person gets angry and attacks you, you give the person what they want, you increase the likelihood they will keep getting angry at you, over time. You reinforce them.

There are two types of reinforcement: **positive** or <u>reward</u> (praise, frequent flyer miles, grades, money, a smile) and **negative** or <u>relief</u> such as aspirin for a headache, stopping nagging when you clean up the room, the noise stops when you buckle your seatbelt. <u>Your target behavior is a negative reinforcer!</u> Negative reinforcement can be really hard to understand and is easily confused with punishment. This link has some examples of negative reinforcers: http://www.educateautism.com/behavioural-principles/examples-of-negative-reinforcement.html.

We can **shape** successive approximations of the desired behavior. For instance, we applaud someone's efforts to hit the tennis ball even if they aren't very skilled at it. Every time they come close, we applaud - this is shaping.

Timing counts: reinforce right away. If you're working with a tennis coach, you want to hear, "Good shot!" after you've made a good shot. You don't want the coaching session to be over and then be told, "Remember that 14th swing? That was a good shot."

The homework for this week is IPE Worksheet 14 on page 194. It says, "In advance, identify the behavior you want to increase [in yourself or someone else] and the reinforcer [positive or negative] you will use." It's really important that you actually try the behavior change strategies we learned this week. Next week, we'll talk about punishment and extinction to decrease undesirable behavior.

Wishing you a week filled with positive reinforcement.

Dear DBT skills class,

This week we continued learning strategies to change your own or someone else's behavior. Last week, we talked about how to increase <u>desirable</u> behavior; this uses **reinforcement** (positive or negative). To decrease or stop <u>undesired</u> behaviors we use **extinction** or **punishment**. This is found on IPE Handouts #21 and 22, on pages 162-163.

Extinction is a way of reducing a behavior by removing its reinforcer. So you start ignoring your kid who is pestering you for candy in the grocery store line (you've removed the reinforcer of attention and the reinforcer of candy). Of course there may be an extinction burst – that kid will escalate first before giving up. Or let's say that your child throws a tantrum when you tell him it's time for bed. Usually, you give in and let him stay up - that's his reward, or the positive reinforcer. Extinction would be not to give in and not to let him stay up when he throws a tantrum; you have removed the reinforcer. Extinction of his tantrums over time is helped along by reinforcing his efforts not to pitch a fit (remember that this is called **shaping**).

Punishment is what we do to decrease undesirable behavior. Positive punishment means adding something unpleasant in order to decrease a behavior; negative punishment means taking away something desirable, in order to decrease undesirable behavior. If your teenager brings home the family car without a full tank of gas, you can add something "negative" (take out the trash for a week) or take away something "positive" (getting to borrow the car). Research shows that punishment is relatively ineffective and it has to be accompanied by a reinforcer of the desired behavior; it also depends upon you being there to enforce it.

Punishment has to fit the crime, and works best when it is specific and time-limited. Neither punishment nor extinction teaches the person anything new, so it is helpful to reinforce desirable alternative behaviors. For example, you might say at bedtime, "I can see that you're distressed, and I know how hard you're trying not to throw a tantrum. If you are successful, then I'll make your favorite breakfast in the morning." Punishment only works when you're present, which is a problem.

When using any of these strategies (reinforcement, extinction, punishment) it helps to remember that not all consequences are created equal – the value to the person matters. Natural consequences are more effective in the long run than arbitrary ones. A hangover is a natural consequence of drinking too much; being terminated from therapy is a natural consequence of not paying your therapy bill. Behavior learned in one context may not fit another one; we have to learn new behaviors in all relevant contexts. Behaviors that are rewarded at home might not be rewarded at work. This is why we insist you practice.

The homework for this week is IPE Worksheet 15 on page 195. There is a typo on this page, in the instructions. What Linehan meant to write is, "Fill out this sheet whenever you try to decrease your own or someone else's undesirable behavior with punishment or extinction. Look for opportunities (since they occur all the time) to extinguish or punish behavior." It's really important that you actually try the behavior change strategies we learned this week. Next week, we'll be reviewing the entire Interpersonal Effectiveness module.

Dear DBT skills class,

In our last class meeting we reviewed the Interpersonal Effectiveness (IPE) module. We divided the module into three parts.

First, we looked at how to ask for what you want or say "no" and be taken seriously. We all have factors that interfere with our ability to be effective; sometimes these are myths we hold about asking or saying "no". It's essential, before entering into a conversation, to clarify your priorities: your overall objective, relationship goal, and self-respect goal. Whichever of these is most important will determine which set of skills you emphasize. You'll always use some combination of DEAR MAN GIVE FAST but the emphasis changes. Finally, in this part, we learned how to evaluate how intensely to ask or to say "no". DEAR MAN GIVE FAST is, like so much of DBT, an acronym that can be used as a prompt to remind you of the skills to use. D(describe) E(express) A(assert, ask) R(reinforce) M(stay mindful) A(appear confident) N(negotiate) G(gentle manner) I(act interested) V(validate) E(easy does it) F(be fair to yourself and the other person) A(no apologies for asking or refusing) S(stick to your values) T(be truthful).

Next, we reviewed the skills for building, maintaining, or ending relationships. How do you find and get people to like you? Important factors are proximity, similarity, and your conversational skills. Maintaining relationships will call on your Core Mindfulness skills because mindfulness of others (observing, describing, participating, being non-judgmental, one-mindful, and effective) will build closeness with others. The module also talks about how to end destructive or interfering relationships (the difference between the two is on p. 145). Never end a relationship when you are in Emotion Mind! You can use the other IPE skills (DEAR MAN GIVE FAST) to end it, and please put safety first when ending a relationship.

This module also teaches walking the middle path, or balancing acceptance and change. Dialectics are seeming opposites that co-exist; both have kernels of truth. We can practice validation of ourselves and of others by paying attention, reflecting back what was said, paying attention to non-verbal cues and what is not said, and understanding that all behavior is caused. Acknowledge only the valid, never the invalid. To handle invalidation, use the same steps as when practicing validation; try to stay non-defensive. It's also important to acknowledge when we ourselves have said or done something invalid. Finally, there are some highly valid and reliable strategies for changing behavior. We reward or reinforce to increase behavior; we punish or extinguish undesirable behavior. Punishment is not very effective, but if you choose to extinguish, know that there will be an extinction burst, meaning that the behavior will get worse before it disappears. You can shape successive attempts to move toward more desirable behavior by reinforcing (rewarding) each try; think of the "hotter, colder" game.

Your homework is, once again, IPE Worksheets 14 and 15 on pages 194-195.

Skills Reminders for the Emotion Regulation Module

Dear DBT skills class,

This week we began a new module, Emotion Regulation. We reviewed the goals listed on ER Handout #1 (p. 205) to orient ourselves. There are five goals in this module, and each goal will be achieved by the use of one or more specific skills from this module:

Goal #1: Know what "emotion regulation" is (and isn't). Basically, emotion regulation is the ability to control or influence <u>which</u> emotions you have, <u>when</u> you have them, and <u>how</u> you experience or express them. By consciously, deliberately, and intentionally practicing the skills of this module, your ability to regulate your emotions will become automatic.

Goal #2: Understand the emotions you experience. This will entail applying CM skills (observe, describe, etc.) and being able to put names on your emotions. All emotions have a function, a purpose. What is the purpose of this emotion at this time?

Goal #3: Decrease the frequency of unwanted emotions. You'll do this by either preventing them from starting in the first place or by changing them once they start.

Goal #4: Decrease the likelihood of slipping into Emotion Mind, or, once you catch yourself in EM, pull yourself back out. We can reduce our vulnerability to being the victim of our emotions. We can also, once we observe ourselves reacting with high emotional sensitivity, use our ER skills to turn down the volume on the emotion and our response.

Goal #5: Decrease emotional suffering. This means you'll be able to reduce your suffering when painful emotions overcome you, and to manage your extreme emotions so that you don't make things worse.

Please notice that nowhere here is the goal, "Stop having emotions" listed. That's not possible. We have emotions for a reason; we all have them; we cannot un-have them. What we <u>can</u> do is learn to dial down the volume on our emotions, to feel less victimized by them, to manage them more skillfully; in a word, to regulate them.

We also talked about the **function of emotions** (see goal #2, above). What do your emotions do for you? Emotions are hard-wired into us; in fact, they have purposes that help our species survive. There are three primary functions (ER Handout #3, p. 210): to motivate us and organize us to take action; to communicate to and influence other people; and to serve as signals to ourselves to check things out. All emotions are valid, all the time; your emotion in a particular situation may not be justified, however. That is, information about situations that is based on emotions may be inaccurate, and treating emotions as if they were facts can get us into trouble.

Homework for this week: ER Worksheet #2 on page 275 (2a is an example of how to do it) <u>or</u> ER Worksheet #2b on page 277) (2c is an example of how to do it).

Wishing you a good, mindful week.

DBT Reminder: What Makes It So Hard to Regulate Your Emotions?

Dear DBT skills class,

Last class we looked at ER Handouts 4 and 4a (pages 211 and 212). What makes it so hard to regulate your emotions?

Handout 4 lists the things that make it hard to regulate your emotions. One is <u>biological factors</u>. That is, some people are born emotionally sensitive - their physiology and brain chemistry appear to predispose them to difficulty regulating their emotions. Sensitive babies grow up to be sensitive adults. We also know from research that children who have experienced trauma and/or neglect show differences in their brain chemistry from children who did not; they are more likely to experience depression as a result. For many reasons, you may <u>lack the necessary skills</u> (what a good thing you're in DBT, then!). When we are <u>emotionally overloaded</u> it is tremendously hard to dial down the volume, or to turn the emotional thermostat down (which is where the Distress Tolerance skills come in). That's true even if we're willing - but sometimes we are simply <u>unwilling</u> to put in the work to regulate them. Our willfulness says that it's too hard, or we shouldn't have to. It may be that you have <u>environmental reinforcers</u> that encourage your emotional dysregulation. For example, if every time you rage people give you what you want - why would you give up raging? Or if the only way you can be taken seriously is if you cry, it will be very tough for you to learn to regulate sadness. Finally, most of us subscribe to a whole bunch of <u>myths about emotions</u>. Handout 4a lists a number of those myths. Believing in these tall tales makes it very hard to regulate your emotions.

Homework for this week is ER Worksheet #3 on pages 279-280. This asks you to identify myths about emotions that you believe, and to rewrite them in a less judgmental way (that you can still believe). Can't wait to hear what you come up with!

Dear DBT skills class.

Emotions are complex, full-system (brain and body) responses. Changing <u>any</u> part of the system can change the entire response. ER Handout 5 on page 213, the flow chart, goes along with ER Handout 6 (pp. 214-223) and ER Worksheets 4 or 4a on pages 281 or 282. Another possibility is the Wave, which we distributed in class and which is attached to this email.

Characteristics of emotions: They are complex, automatic, and cannot be changed directly (i.e., we can't tell ourselves to feel something and then feel it – or not to feel something and stop feeling it). Emotions are sudden. They rise and fall. They're self-perpetuating – they love themselves. Some are universal.

The model of how emotions work looks like a flow chart. We will teach you skills so that you can change any or all of these factors:

<u>Vulnerability factors</u> (events from the near past or the distant past) - these make us more biologically reactive so when these change, emotions can change.

<u>Prompting event</u> (these are internal or external) - an event is only an event if you're aware of it, so if you don't know about it or you can distract yourself from it, the event will affect you less strongly. In other words, when this changes, your emotion can change.

<u>Interpretation of the prompting event</u> - these are your thoughts, beliefs, the stories you tell yourself about the prompting event. When your interpretation changes, emotions can change.

<u>Biological changes</u> – when emotions fire, several complex biological changes happen very quickly. These include neurochemical changes in your brain, and changes in your nervous system including blood pressure and heart rate. When these change, emotions can change.

<u>Body sensations and urges</u> – emotions are almost always associated with these. For example, sadness tends to produce a tightness in the throat, low energy, and/or emptiness. Anger can result in a sensation of heat, agitation, and/or "seeing red". When body sensations change, emotions can change/decrease in intensity.

<u>Facial expressions and body language</u> – remember that one function of emotions is communication; that's why facial expressions are somewhat hardwired. When facial and body expressions change, emotions can change.

Action – This is another function of emotions. One of the most important tasks in developing is learning to inhibit emotional actions. When actions change, emotions can change.

Emotion names – Evidence shows that naming your feelings is helpful. It's easier to name simple emotions than complex ones. Through naming, emotions can change.

Aftereffects – emotions love themselves. Monitoring the aftereffects of intense emotions can help change subsequent emotions. Once you know that intense emotions narrow attention and increase sensitivity to cues for the same emotion, you can remind yourself to check the facts. Knowing you may be seeing things through the lenses of the emotion you are trying to change rather than the lenses of present reality can be helpful.

Practice is to read through ER Handout #6 on pp. 214-223 (in which each of 10 emotions is tracked through the steps of the flow chart) and to complete ER Worksheets 4 or 4a on pages 281-282. You can choose to use the Wave instead if you prefer. In any case, please be sure to track an emotion more than once. This is all about gathering data.

DBT Reminder: Check the Facts

Dear DBT skills class,

This week we learned the first skill in the ER module: **Check the Facts** (ER Handouts #8 and 8a, pages 228-229). As you will remember from the Model of Emotions (the flow chart or the Wave), every prompting event triggers a cascade of effects; the first one is our thought about the event. This is our interpretation, belief, a myth, or the story we tell ourselves about the event. It's rarely the event itself that causes us a problem; the problem comes because we insist upon having an opinion about the event. Of course, once we have made our interpretation and have an emotional response to it, that emotion itself can be a new prompting event that triggers further interpretations. So the skill of checking the facts is one way we can intervene in the cascade of effects, so as to down-regulate our emotions.

There are six steps to this skill. The six steps on the handout (#8) correspond exactly to the steps on ER Worksheet #5, (pp. 285-286). <u>First</u>, you have to know what emotion you're trying to change. "Bad" is not an emotion. "Upset" is not an emotion, and neither is "stressed." Take a look at ER Handout #6 (pages 214-223) for the list of 10 primary emotions and some events that can prompt them. <u>Second</u>, describe the event that prompted the emotion in non-judgmental terms. Stick to the facts. Avoid all-or-nothing terms and generalizations. Imagine you're describing what happened to someone who doesn't speak English very well (this will help keep your explanations short and to the point). <u>Next</u>, challenge your interpretation of the event. The act of listing alternative interpretations can decrease your emotion's intensity. Are there any other possible interpretations? If you have to, borrow someone else's Wise Mind to do this step. <u>Fourth</u>, ask yourself if you're assuming there is a threat present. A threat is any negative outcome. Label the threat: what is it you assume will happen, exactly? How likely is it that the threat will occur? Are there any other possible outcomes instead? <u>Step five</u> is to ask yourself, "What is the catastrophe I am assuming will occur now?" Imagine the catastrophe really occurring and then plan how you will respond to it. <u>Finally</u>, ask yourself if your emotion is justified; that is, does your emotion fit the facts of the situation? We say that all feelings are valid, all the time, but that some feelings are not justified because they either don't fit the facts of the situation, or they do fit the facts but are much too big for the situation - they're out of proportion to it. The intensity and duration of an emotion are justified if it is likely that the outcome you fear will, in fact, take place; if the outcome is very important to you; and if the emotion is effective for coping with that outcome right now. ER Handout 8a has some examples of emotions that are justified: they fit the facts of the situation.

As with every skill, this is time-consuming at first; it takes practice. Sometimes, just putting a name to your emotion takes time - but it may also pull you out of Emotion Mind and closer to Reason Mind. The second step, describing the prompting event non-judgmentally, can really down-regulate your emotion but learning how to do it isn't intuitive for many of us. Listing alternate interpretations is a great way to practice dialectics (seeing more than one truth in a situation). If you have done each of those first three steps completely and thoroughly, you will probably have regulated your emotion considerably. If not, keep going.

For homework, please complete ER Worksheet # 5 (pp. 285-286).

Wishing you a good, mindful week.

Dear DBT skills class,

In our last class, we spent time with three handouts: #9, #10, and #11 in the ER module (pp. 230, 231, and 232-238). Some of the skills in this module are about keeping you from getting into Emotion Mind in the first place; the others are about pulling you back from the brink when you're about to go into EM. To do that, you have to change your unwanted emotions. There are three ways to do that: 1) check the facts; 2) problem-solve; or 3) opposite-to-the-emotion action (OTEA). Both Problem-Solving and OTEA require that you first use last week's skill, Check the Facts. Having done that, ER Handout #9 is all about how to decide whether to use Opposite Action (the next skill in the module) or Problem-solving (a later skill).

ER Handout #10 summarizes **Opposite to the Emotion Action (OTEA)**; this is the skill to use when either your emotions don't fit the facts or when acting on your emotions, even if they fit, wouldn't be effective.. The principle here is that you'll identify what it is that makes you angry, anxious, sad, ashamed, etc., and then allow yourself to be exposed to that trigger without acting on your urges. Acting in the way that is opposite to the action urge of your emotion is highly effective at changing the emotion.

There are seven steps. 1) identify and name the emotion you want to change (use Handout #6 from this module if you're stuck). Sometimes just doing so will reduce the emotion's intensity. 2) Check the facts to see if your emotion fits the facts. Use Handouts 8 and 8a from this module. 3) Identify and describe your action urges. 4) Ask your Wise Mind whether acting on or even expressing this emotion will be effective right now. If the answer is yes, go back to Handout #9: you can be mindful of the emotion, act on it, or use the skill of Problem-Solving. If the answer is no (that is, if acting on your emotion won't be effective right now) or if your emotion doesn't fit the facts (step 2) then use Handout #11 to identify possible opposite actions for your action urges. Let this skill do the work of reducing the emotion's intensity and duration. 6) Do OTEA all the way - doing it halfway won't be effective. 7) Repeat until your emotion changes or decreases in intensity to a more tolerable level.

Handout #11 lists each of the primary emotions and some action urges for each, as well as suggested opposite actions for each. It's important, though, to personalize this: you have to act opposite to <u>your</u> action urges as they present themselves, not to someone else's. If you're angry, taking a time out or changing your posture might not fit your particular action urges. Maybe you need a different action to do this skill.

For homework, please complete ER Worksheet #7 on page 288. You might want to use ER Worksheet #6 (p. 287) to decide whether you want to change the emotion or if Problem-Solving will be a more effective skill. If you decide that you do want to change that emotion then use ER Worksheet #7. We're confident you'll have plenty of opportunities to use both worksheets.

Next class, we'll be continuing to work with OTEA, but we'll focus exclusively on how to do Opposite Action for shame and guilt. These emotions are more complicated and figuring out whether your shame is justified can be daunting.

Dear DBT skills class,

This week we finished learning about Opposite to the Emotion Action (OTEA) for those most corrosive of feelings: guilt and shame. We have attached here a matrix for deciding if your guilt and/or shame are justified or unjustified. This accompanies pages 239 and 240 in the manual. On page 239, we labeled the two sections A and B; on page 240 they are A and C.

Remember that there are three possible ways to down-regulate your emotions: 1) check the facts; 2) solve the problem; or 3) act opposite to the emotion's urging. We <u>always</u> start by checking the facts.

We define guilt as what we feel because of something we've done (or failed to do); shame, on the other hand, is about a personal characteristic. Another way to think of it: Guilt says, "I made a mistake" but shame says, "I <u>am</u> a mistake."

Use the matrix to help you determine if your guilt or shame are justified or unjustified. We used an example of borrowing a friend's blouse, then ruining it in the washing machine. You might feel guilt (oops, I made a mistake!) as well as shame (oh no, I'm such an idiot, and she's going to be so mad!). We use the skill of **Check the Facts** to generate other possible interpretations of the prompting event: maybe I tossed a whole lot of clothes in the washer and didn't see the blouse; maybe she hated that blouse; maybe the blouse didn't look well on her anyway. We have no idea if these are true, but they are possible, so our guilt and our shame may not fit the facts. Even if they fit the facts, the intensity may not be appropriate; or the shame may cause us to avoid our friend, which isn't an effective way to maintain a friendship. It may be that the guilt is justified but the shame isn't (because it's ineffective). Using our matrix, we see that we're in box B. Page 239, at the bottom, tells you how to use OTEA all-the-way, then.

Here's another example: if you're in AA and NA but you believe in the value of medical marijuana, this would put you in conflict with a great many members of the AA and NA fellowships but wouldn't violate your WM values: this is box C (and see page 240, at the bottom).

Once you have figured out whether your shame is an A, B, C, or D, turn to pages 239 and 240 and find the appropriate box. Follow the directions there to practice the opposite action to shame. When both our shame and our guilt are unjustified (A) we definitely want to do the opposite of those action urges (directions at the top of pages 239 and 240). Even if they're both justified (D), the emotions may not be effective so we may need some OTEA.

Please do ER Worksheet 7, once again, and bring it in to share when we next meet.

Wishing you a shame-free, guilt-free week.

DBT Reminder: Problem-Solving

Dear DBT skills class,

Remember that there are three ways to change unwanted emotions: 1) **check the facts**; 2) **problem-solve**; or 3) **opposite-to-the-emotion action (OTEA)**. The skill of **problem-solving** can get us out of Emotion Mind (EM). When your emotion is justified - when the problem really is the situation - changing the situation may be the best way to change your emotion (that is, to decrease its intensity). We followed a step-by-step algorithm (just like cooking from a recipe) to use this skill. The handout for this is #12 on page 241; the worksheet is #8, on page 289.

In order to use this skill, we first have to acknowledge that a problem exists. We state the problem (just the facts) and our interpretation of the problem (our beliefs, stories, thoughts, ideas about the problem). What makes this situation a problem for you? Why is it so terrible? What are the obstacles to solving it? Be as specific as you possibly can be. Our next step is to check our facts, which may mean getting a reality check from another person. If we cannot physically do that (or if it would be very difficult even though we have the willingness) we might assess probabilities: how likely is it that the story I'm telling myself is correct? How probable are the consequences, obstacles, and my interpretations? Here, what we want to do is make sure that the problem really is a problem - that you're not responding to your interpretation of a prompting event, but to an actual event and actual obstacles. Remember that your interpretation may be a myth or a story you've told yourself, not factual.

At this point, we will realize that either our interpretation of the prompting event (the thing that got us upset in the first place) is incorrect, and that we need to change it; or we will realize that there really is a problem here. For instance, either our friend was not really mad at us, as we thought, and we need to change our interpretation of the expression on her face; or she really is mad at us, just as we believed, in which case we have a problem that requires a solution.

If your facts are not correct, then go back and do the first step again: describe the problem. Remember that using the skill of Check the Facts may be enough to reduce the intensity of your distress.

What if there really is a problem to be solved? Step by step, then, we figure out what a solution would look like. What has to happen in order for you to feel "better"? How will you know the problem has been solved? Keep it simple, here. Then brainstorm as many ways as you can think of to achieve that solution. In brainstorming, all ideas are fair game, no matter whether there is a likelihood you'll use them or not. It's also really important <u>not</u> to act impulsively but instead to work your way through all the steps of this skill. Pick two ideas that are possible to do and that are likely to help you reach your acceptable solution. List all the baby steps required to carry out each of those ideas. You may want to do the pros and cons of choosing one approach over the other. Pick one, then try it out! What happened? Did you solve your problem? Did the intensity of your emotion decrease? If not, go back to the list of possible solutions you brainstormed, and do it all again.

Please try this out this week on a problem. Do your best to follow the steps outlined on the handout and on ER worksheet #8 on page 289. Problem-solving is one of the core skills of this module and requires practice and conscious effort. We look forward to hearing your stories!

DBT Reminder: VITALS

Dear DBT skills class,

This week we're reviewing OTEA and Problem-solving, which gives us the opportunity to learn a new acronym: **VITALS**. We started with the review, which is on ER Handout #13 (pp. 242-243).

Problem-solving is the skill to use when the emotion is justified (that is, it fits the facts and is right-sized to them). Remembering that every emotion has a function (or more than one), one way to problem-solve is to act on your emotion. If the function of the emotion is to motivate us to take action, then taking action will, in fact, solve the problem. An example here is a tsunami: the emotion is fear, the and action urge is to run. Please do that; we want you to. In this case, acting on your emotion is solving the problem. Sometimes, though, acting on your emotion's urge may only provide a temporary solution (think of the rat in the kitchen: running out of the room reduces your fear, but it doesn't solve the problem - you still have a rat in your kitchen). So avoiding the problem can be a type of problem-solving, under some circumstances - but not all. You're going to need to problem-solve a permanent solution to that rat (call an exterminator, set a trap, get a cat, move away). An example of when avoiding the problem is a type of problem-solving over the long term would be leaving an abusive relationship.

When your emotion isn't justified (it doesn't fit the facts, or its intensity or duration are too big for the facts) the skill to use is OTEA. ER Handout #13 reviews examples of how to apply this skill to specific emotions.

It can be a real challenge, though, to apply OTEA. We like the acronym VITALS for the step-by-step process of using this skill. (A handout is attached here).

V = **Validate** yourself. <u>Of course</u> you don't want to go back in the kitchen where the rat is, <u>of course</u> you're angry at that person, <u>of course</u>... your feelings are valid. There's a reason for them.

I = **Imagine** yourself using the skill: approaching, smiling, being non-judgmental, whatever the skillful behavior is, imagine yourself doing it.

T = **Take** small steps. Break the task down into baby steps. If you don't want to go to your therapy session, just get your shoes on and find your car keys. That's all (for now).

A = **Applaud** yourself. Cheerlead yourself, encourage your efforts.

L = **Lighten** the load. Remind yourself of what you're going to achieve when you've used this skill: decreasing fear, or shame, or anger; avoiding having to apologize; avoiding hating yourself.

S = **Sweeten** the pot. Reward yourself! Add something during the process of using the skill or when you're done that rewards you for your accomplishment.

For homework this week, please use (once again) ER Worksheets #6, 7, and/or 8 on pages 287-289. We'll see you in class.

Dear DBT skills class,

We have been learning how to reduce unpleasant, uncomfortable, or afflictive emotions (anger, sadness, shame/guilt, or fear). We can do this in several ways: by changing the thoughts that always come before feelings (Check the Facts); by solving the problem that gave rise to the discomfort (Problem-Solving); or by using a series of steps that get us to take action that is the opposite of our Emotion Mind urges (OTEA). It's obviously more desirable, though, if we can <u>avoid</u> those afflictive emotions in the first place, and that's what the next few weeks are all about. How can we reduce our vulnerability to being in Emotion Mind?

The next set of skills in the module (ABC PLEASE) is designed to increase your resilience and decrease emotional distress. We started learning the skill of **Accumulating Positives**, which can be done in three ways: a) we can increase daily positive experiences (short-term); b) we can pay attention to the positive events in our daily lives and be unmindful of negative events (short-term); or c) we can build up to the life that we want by taking a small step, every single day, that will get us there (long-term). This week we talked about the short-term ways to use the skill.

Increasing positive events leads to an increase in pleasant emotions and a decrease in our vulnerability to unpleasant emotions. So we're going to increase the positive emotions in our life by increasing the events that prompt positive emotions, including love, joy, pride, self-confidence, calmness, serenity, and contentment (ER Handout #15, p. 248). Do one pleasant activity every day - if you can't think of anything, try something from the Pleasant Events list in ER Handout #16 starting on page 249. The goal is to incorporate these into your life on a regular basis, which adds up to a more pleasant, satisfying experience. The more that we can build contentment and fun into our life, the less difficult it becomes to tolerate the otherwise irritating or bothersome aspects. Sometimes just stepping outside, breathing in the cool air, feeling the sun, and hearing the birds can provide a lift.

This skill takes lots of time and patience. It's call <u>Accumulate</u> Positives because you won't get the benefits by just doing it one time. It may require you to use OTEA and/or Problem-Solving to make it happen. It may be necessary to both:

- Be mindful of positive experiences. Having a massage is not relaxing or pleasurable unless you allow yourself to relax and attend to the pleasure involved. Use your mindfulness skills to focus your attention on the positive events — small and large. If/when your mind wanders to negative terrain, coax it back (again and again as needed).

- Be <u>un</u>mindful of the negative. Notice if you find yourself sabotaging your enjoying by questioning whether you deserve to enjoy yourself (you do!); worrying about what you should be doing (everyone can afford to schedule in pleasurable down time); or worrying about when it will end (rather than enjoying yourself in the moment for what it is). You'll probably find that the DT skills of Pushing Away Thoughts and Substituting other Thoughts will be helpful, here.

For homework, we are using ER Worksheet #9 or #10; these are found on pages 293 and 295. Every day, accumulate a positive; and every day, be mindful of the positives and unmindful of the negatives (those stories we may tell ourselves). In a nutshell, your homework is to seek out pleasure and fun.

Dear DBT skills class,

This week we turned our attention from how to use the skill of **Accumulate Positives** in our daily lives, to how to accumulate positive emotions in the long term by living according to our values. We are on ER Handouts #17 and 18, on pages 252-255.

The bad news first: if you want to be happier, you will have to make changes. Always seeking things that make us feel better <u>now</u> can get in the way of building permanent positive events into our lives. So this skill is like putting pennies into a piggy bank.

The good news is: You can do this, if you take it step by step. There are many, many obstacles to accumulating positives over the long term (not knowing what you want, depression, living in Emotion Mind, an unwillingness to accept that life isn't fair). You are going to have to make a decision to do something different than what you have previously done.

Next (step 2) identify what you value. What's important to you in your life? What are your highest priorities in life - what really matters to you? You can look at ER Handout #18 for some suggestions. Values do not have an endpoint, like getting your diploma or a good night's sleep (those are both goals). Values are timeless. Values can change over the course of your life. Research has shown that simply naming one's values can reduce anxiety and depression.

Step 3 is to choose one <u>value</u> to work on <u>right now</u>. It might be your highest priority, or it might be low-hanging fruit. Step 4: list lots of specific <u>goals</u> related to this value. If your value is to have close and satisfying relationships with others, a specific goal might be to make one new friend. If your value is to care for the environment, a specific goal might be to replace all the bulbs in your home with LEDs.

In Step 5, choose one <u>goal</u> to work on right now. In Step 6, identify all the baby steps needed to get you to that goal. If your goal was to make one new friend, what are all the steps you'd have to take to achieve that goal? For example, join a club or group of some kind, introduce yourself to members of that club, smile at members of the club, make eye contact with members, talk to one person at each club meeting, invite one person for coffee after the meeting, etc. If a step seems too big, break it down again. I'd be breaking down "join a club or group of some kind" into smaller steps, because how are you going to find such a group? Go online, look at bulletin boards at the library or church, ask people in class what groups they belong to. I'd go even smaller: turn on the computer (to get online). Step 7: take one step now!

ER Worksheets #11 or 11a or 11b are your homework. #11 walks you through these steps in a very linear fashion. Worksheet #11a is briefer but it's the same material. Worksheet #11b is a diary format. These worksheets start on p. 296.

Finally, remember that the homework is not designed to produce an immediate result. Change takes time and persistent practice. Go back to the good news, above: you can do this if you take it step by step. And further good news: accumulating positive emotions by achieving goals that allow you to live according to your values <u>will</u> give you a life worth living! We promise.

Dear DBT skills class,

Feeling competent and adequately prepared to deal with difficult situations reduces our vulnerability to Emotion Mind and increases resiliency. This week we looked at ER Handout #19 on page 256. The skill of **Building Mastery** means doing anything that leaves you feeling competent, confident and capable. Mastery makes one resistant to depression.

Plan to do something every day to build a sense of accomplishment. Plan for success and choose to do something a little bit hard, but not impossible. Attached is a list of some ways you might think about building mastery. It's like muscle-building: you must practice these activities every single day to build mastery. If you practice Spanish daily for a year, at the end of a year you will have built mastery. ¡Te sientes orgullosa! When you speak Spanish, or even when you think about speaking in Spanish, you might feel strong and competent, which will improve your mood and will make you believe you can tackle other difficult tasks, as well. The beauty of this is that when something happens that leaves us feeling discouraged or deflated, we can remind ourselves of our mastery of speaking in Spanish, and move away from EM.

We also learned how to **Cope Ahead** with situations that are likely to fast-track us into Emotion Mind. One instinct, when we feel anxious or threatened, is to avoid. We want to run away. We try to avoid thinking about the pending situation, and we try to avoid feeling anxiety, anger, sadness, or shame/guilt. Then we get into the situation, feel overwhelmed by the surge of thoughts and feelings, and may react unskillfully, entering Emotion Mind quickly.

Rumination is full of "what if?" and "this is horrible" while Coping Ahead is full of "here is how I will handle that." Where rumination gives us the illusion of being in control, Coping Ahead actually teaches us to make a plan so that we will be in control - of our emotions, thoughts, and behaviors - in difficult situations.

DBT suggests that you sit down and imagine yourself in the challenging situation. Go into as much detail as you can. Step by step, walk through the situation in your mind. Imagine yourself using your skills to stay out of Emotion Mind. Now... imagine a problem or obstacle; what is the worst thing that could happen? How will you cope? What skills can you use when this awful thing happens? And what happens next? You're afraid that it will all go horribly wrong - OK, what if it does? How will you respond? A helpful hint here is to be as specific as possible about the obstacles and your response to them.

By using the skill of Coping Ahead, you will be prepared to apply your skills to the problematic situation. You'll be ready to deal with any problems that arise. (You may recognize that this is like the "I" of IMPROVE the moment: Imagine yourself coping skillfully with the distressing event. In this case, we are using the skill proactively, not reactively.) There is also an element of the Emotion Regulation skill of Problem-Solving here, because you are anticipating problems that might occur and getting yourself prepared to deal with them, ahead of time. It does help to be very specific about what, exactly, the problem is that you're trying to solve.

Try this out at least once this week. Use ER homework sheets #12 and 13 on pages 301 and 302. We are eager to hear what you bring in as your experiences.

Dear DBT skills class,

In the last class we went over handouts that addressed taking care of your body, since a healthy body is less emotionally vulnerable. ER Handout 20 on page 257 addressed the PLEASE skills, and ER Handouts 20a and 20b (page 258-259) addressed ways to improve your sleep.

PL: treat **Physical iLlness**. People are more prone to uncomfortable emotions when they are physically ill. The PL skill involves seeing your doctor when you are sick, maintaining your health, and taking your medications as prescribed.

E: balance **Eating**. Eating too much or too little can lead to emotional dysregulation. Studies have shown that eating too few calories also leads to distractibility, dysphoria, increased emotional dysregulation, and bingeing. Studies are now looking into the impact that fluctuating glucose levels have on mood and how simple sugars in the diet may contribute to inflammatory processes that may be linked to depression.

A: Avoid mood-altering drugs, such as alcohol and illicit drugs. Some people are able to consume alcohol in moderation, but some cannot. Some people also find that they need to avoid caffeine because it leads to anxiety, irritability, or insomnia.

S: Balance **sleep**, aiming for 7 to 8 hours per night. Research shows that too little sleep is a risk factor for mood disorder episodes, it adversely impacts cognitive functioning, and it can contribute to substance abuse relapse and suicide. Too much or too little sleep also increases mortality rates.

E: Get **exercise**. Regular exercise can be as useful as medication in mild depression, and consistent exercise can build mastery.

Handout 20a is a nightmare protocol that is based on IRT, Imagery Rehearsal Therapy. If you suffer with nightmares, take this to your individual therapist to work on. If practiced frequently, changes are usually seen in a few weeks. Studies have shown a reduction in nightmare frequency or intensity, and some people actually stop having the nightmare.

Handout 20b gives sleep hygiene tips. People with insomnia need a consistent routine prior to bed time as well as consistent lights-out and wake times. Remember that viewing TV, computer screens, and electronics one hour before bedtime suppresses melatonin production, and adequate melatonin levels are necessary for the onset of sleep.

Homework is ER Worksheet #14 on page 303. Use ER Worksheet 14a (pages 304-306) to target nightmares, and use 14b (page 307) if necessary to improve your sleep hygiene.

Wishing you a physically healthy week.

Dear DBT skills class,

Last class we started the next section of the ER module, which is a special set of skills for managing really difficult emotions. The first of these skills is **Mindfulness of the Current Emotion** (ER Handouts 21 and 22, pages 263-264)

Why would you want to do this? Wouldn't it be better <u>not</u> to be aware of our unpleasant, afflictive feelings? Research shows that suppressing emotions increases suffering: "what we resist, persists". Whatever we try to suppress or block will come back stronger than ever - and often not at a convenient time! Further, avoiding your emotions interferes with your ability to use just about every other skill in this module.

The good news is that you already have most of the skills you'll need to practice this skill effectively: the skills of **Observe**, **Describe**, and **Non-judgmentally**.

1) Observe your emotions. Be mindful of your experience. This allows you to distance yourself from emotions while you are experiencing them. Experience the emotion like a wave. Let it wash over you -- resist the urge to ignore it, push it away, deny it, or hold on to it. Try naming the emotion(s) you feel. The more able you are to observe your emotion, and tolerate it, the less vulnerable you will be to it. Please don't try to do this for more than 30 seconds at a time - that's plenty.

2) Try to focus on one particular quality of your experience, such as the physical sensation. For example, if you are experiencing anxiety or anger, focus on the physical experience of feeling these feelings (rather than becoming involved in self talk that may be fueling the emotions, such as getting stuck on why you may feel this way, or the content of your worries). Observe and describe your body sensations.

3) Remind yourself that you are separate from the emotion. In this way, you can choose how to respond to an emotion, rather than being driven by it. Noting that things do and will change can also be helpful.

4) As best you can, accept (or even love) the emotion. Loving emotions is equivalent to validating them, and ourselves for having them. All emotions have a function, even the uncomfortable ones. Don't assume that what you're feeling is irrational or "wrong."

The homework is ER Worksheet #15 on page 311. Try as many of the steps – and check them off – as you can. We urge you to try this more than once during this week. You're learning that uncomfortable emotions are not a disaster; you're learning that you don't have to be controlled by any myths about emotions, such as, "I can't afford to feel X because if I do I won't be able to stop." We look forward to hearing your experiences.

Wishing you each a peaceful and mindful week.

Dear DBT skills class,

This week we used ER Handout #23, "Managing Extreme Emotions" and ER Handout #24, "Troubleshooting Emotion Regulation: What do to when your skills don't work". These are on pages 265-267, and the homework is ER Worksheet #16 on page 312.

What should you do if your emotional arousal is very high, you are completely dysregulated, and you just can't figure out what skills to use or how to use them? First, use **Observe** and **Describe** to take your emotional temperature: What is happening to your thoughts, feelings, and body sensations? Second, remain **Non-Judgmental** about your emotional arousal. Next, **Check the Facts**: Are you really "falling apart"? It's always worth discerning, here, if the problem is willfulness.

If you really, truly, are unable to think of a skill, you can of course call your therapist. They will very likely suggest that you start with some skills from the Distress Tolerance module. Then practice **Mindfulness of the Current Emotion** (ER Handout #22, from last week). Finally, use any other ER skills, such as **Opposite Action, Accumulate Positives, or Build Mastery**.

What happens if you are so deep into EM that the skills just won't work? We used Handout #24 to answer this question. Here are the steps to take:

a) Check your **PLEASE** skills: you may be extra vulnerable to EM right now. Fix what you can (e.g., eat, sleep, take medications as prescribed) and try the skills again.

b) Check your skills: Ask if you have followed instructions exactly, without skimping. Have you skipped any steps? Are you using the skills mindfully?

c) Check for anything that may be reinforcing you to stay in EM. Maybe the emotion is doing exactly what it is supposed to (your anger is causing others to do what you want them to do), in which case it's being reinforced and will be very tough to regulate. You might choose a new reinforcer. Even though the emotion has a purpose, and is serving its purpose, it may still be so uncomfortable that it's getting in your way. What are the **Pros and Cons** of letting go of the emotion, or dialing it down, at this time? Use ER Worksheet #1 for this.

d) Check your mindfulness: are you putting in the time and attention necessary? Are you using **Participate, Effectiveness, Radical Acceptance**, and **Willingness**?

e) If you are too distressed to use complex skills, go for simpler ones, such as any of the Distress Tolerance (Crisis Survival) skills, especially **TIPP**, and do them exactly as written. Can the problem you are worrying about be solved <u>right now</u>? It's not that your daughter got her tongue pierced or that you and your husband had a fight about the bills. The problem that can be solved <u>right now</u> is more along the lines of: I want to hurt myself; I want to drink; I can't stop worrying. Once we can figure out what the immediate problem is, we're more likely to be able to apply skills effectively. Use the **Problem-Solving** skill (Handout #12) or practice **Mindfulness of Current Emotion** (Handout #22);

e) Are you invalidating your emotion, trying to use force of will to get rid of it? Maybe a myth about emotions is getting in your way! Worksheet #3 will help you here.

Use Worksheet #16 on page 312 to regulate your emotions. Linehan says, "Food doesn't nourish your body if you don't eat it; skills won't work if you don't practice them mindfully." We're guessing you'll have lots of opportunity to practice this week!

Dear DBT skills class,

We have just reviewed the entire Emotion Regulation (ER) module and the skills it includes. The thing to remember about emotions is that modifying any part of the emotional system will have an effect on the emotion. That's <u>any</u> part. Specific DBT skills are aimed at specific components of emotions. ER Handout #25 on page 268 presents this; it builds on ER Handout #5 (the Model of Emotions, page 213) and shows you which specific skills address which specific part of the emotional system. We also used a graph (attached) as a means to review what we've learned. It comes in two forms: a picture and with words.

Arousal (becoming dysregulated) happens over time. Before we even get to the trigger, there are skills we can use to reduce our vulnerability: **PLEASE, Accumulate Positives, Build Mastery**, and **Cope Ahead**. When the trigger happens, our thoughts precede the emotional dysregulation. **Checking the Facts** is useful because if we check the facts and determine that what we are thinking is a judgment and not a fact, changing it will change the emotion.

If we intervene soon thereafter we will not get over-aroused. A skill that you might find useful here is **Opposite to the Emotion Action**. If we don't do anything (and sometimes even if we do) we will head for an uncomfortable zone. Here, we are having certain beliefs/thoughts/interpretations - and they may be quite insistent: "This is a disaster...", "What if....?" You can intervene by looking at Emotion Regulation Handout #4 (p. 211) to see if any of your insistent thoughts/beliefs/interpretations are actually emotion myths. Try rewriting your myth in a way that triggers your Emotion Mind less <u>and</u> in a way that you are apt to believe. If we remain dysregulated, we cross over into the intolerable zone where our action urges are extremely strong. Some of those urges give us time to think about skills to use (for example, over-spending or over-working will); others do not (e.g., yelling or ruminating won't).

At this point we have two choices. One is natural recovery. If we do nothing, the urge will eventually pass (whether we act on it or we don't), and although it may take us a long time to return to our baseline, we will get there eventually. The other choice is to use our skills. If we do this, we will recover more quickly. We may need to use some of the crisis survival strategies, aka Distress Tolerance skills, first, before we can use more complicated skills from the ER module. **TIPP** can be a good skill here - it tends to work quite quickly. Using **Mindfulness of the Current Emotion** is also likely to be effective (it's a wave, watch it come and go).

Of course it would be wonderful if we could avoid the events that prompt afflictive emotions - or at least reduce their frequency. **Problem-Solving** is a helpful skill for that. But we are unlikely to be successful using Problem-Solving when we are already highly aroused. Again, try using Distress Tolerance skills such as **TIPP**, or **Mindfulness of the Current Emotion** to decrease your distress, then try more complex skills such as **Problem-Solving**.

For homework this week, please choose one incident and use the graph handouts to write up exactly what happens. We think you'll find that answering the questions on the "word" version will help you learn a lot about what happened, what skills were most/less useful in that situation, how long recovery took, what skills you already use that help, and any new skills you may want to add to your repertoire.

Skills Reminders for the Distress Tolerance Module

DBT Reminder: Intro to Distress Tolerance (DT) and STOP skill

Dear DBT skills class,

This week we started the Distress Tolerance module. These are the skills to use in order to survive a crisis without hurting yourself, hurting someone else, or making the situation worse.

The goals of this module, in addition to surviving crises, are to accept reality as it is in this moment; and to be at peace and content, no matter the circumstances we find ourselves in. These skills are not intended for daily use - life is not all crisis. In the long run, acceptance and problem-solving will be needed. These skills carry us through until we are emotionally balanced enough to use more challenging skills.

By definition, a crisis is short-term, highly stressful, and produces urges (to use drugs, to hurt yourself, to pop someone, to overspend) and a feeling of demand (the project must be done now, the bills must be paid now, you have to talk to the person now). The DT skills are used when you want to act out of EM but doing so will make things worse; EM is overwhelming you and you need to stick with your skills; you feel overwhelmed but still have to take care of business; or your emotional arousal is very high but your problem can't be solved right now.

Key to your use of these skills is to remember that you may not "feel better" after using them. That's not what they promise; the promise is that you will have survived the crisis without hurting yourself, hurting someone else, or making it worse. Often we use the DT skills to hang on until we have reduced emotional dysregulation enough that we can start to use the more complex skills from the other modules.

The first skill in this module is STOP, found on DT Handout #4, p. 327. It's a way to decrease reactivity. **S** = **Stop**! Freeze! Don't move a muscle! The idea here is that <u>you</u> are in control, not your emotions or urges. **T** = **Take** a step back. You might even do this literally, but be sure to do it in your mind, getting a bit of distance from the crisis for just a moment. **O** = **Observe**. Fortunately, you already know how to do this, from the CM module. Notice what is going on both inside you (thoughts, feelings, and body sensations) and outside you (in your immediate environment). Gather relevant facts. **P** = **Proceed** mindfully, that is, deliberately, with intention. Ask your Wise Mind, What do I want from this situation? What are my goals?

Here's an example of when you might use this skill: You're crossing the street and don't notice a car coming. The driver stops the car, gets out, starts cursing at you, and jabs your shoulder with her finger. Your urge is to jab her back; you know, though, that doing so would escalate the situation and get you in trouble. You use STOP to (literally) take a step back and avoid confrontation.

The homework for this week is DT Worksheets 2 or 2a, on pages 372 and 373. We look forward to hearing how you side-step crisis events.

DBT Reminder: Pros & Cons

Dear DBT skills class,

This week we are focusing on the skill of Pros and Cons, Handout #5 in the DT module (p. 328). We'll identify all of the positive and negative aspects of resisting urges to use crisis behaviors (using skills instead) _and_ of acting on urges (using crisis behaviors instead of skills).

The first step is to define the behavior of yours that you want to address (such as urges to stay in bed all day, binge eat, hide out from friends, drink/smoke).This may be your familiar means of not facing distressing thoughts or feelings. Other words for "pros" are: advantages, benefits, upside. Other words for "cons" include: risks, downside, cost. As we did in class, develop a list of pros and cons for _engaging_ in the behavior (acting on the urge) and another set for _not_ engaging in the behavior (resisting the urge, which means using skills). This will generate a 2x2 table. Pick something meaningful for you and write out your lists, considering both short and long-term effects. Take your time and think this through.

The next step is to read, read, read over your lists. Practice so that you can bring your lists to mind automatically. This will be helpful the next time you are in a crisis.

We suggest that you apply this skill proactively to every single one of your crisis behaviors. That way, you'll be prepared the next time you're in EM. This skill pulls in Reason Mind through the writing of the four lists (or filling in four boxes).

For homework, use DT Worksheet 3 _or_ 3a (p. 374 _or_ p. 375) for one of your usual go-to crisis behaviors and create the pros and cons lists for that behavior. Worksheet 3 and Worksheet 3a are the same - just in different formats. You get to choose which makes more sense to you. We also asked the question, How will you remember to use this skill, next time you feel urges? Answering the question is part of your homework.

Wishing you each a skillful week.

Dear DBT skills class,

The next skill up in the Distress Tolerance module is one that helps us change our biological response very quickly, thereby decreasing emotional arousal. We use the acronym TIPP to help remind us about this skill. We are on Handouts 6, 6a, 6b, and 6c of the DT module; that's pages 329 - 332.

As you'll remember if you were with us for the ER module, events lead to thoughts which lead to changes in our body chemistry which then lead to feelings. Therefore, one way to intervene is to change our body chemistry. We have three options: 1) change the body **Temperature**. Fill a bowl with ice cubes and water, hold your breath, and plunge your face in up to your ears. Or you can hold an ice pack over your eyes while holding your breath, put a cold washcloth on your face or neck, or splash cold water on your face. 2) **Intense** exercise can help us manage revved-up thoughts and feelings (such as anger, fear, or shame/guilt). Some people even schedule their ruminating for their exercise time. They don't allow themselves to ruminate at any other time of day. This is called "prescribing the symptom." Try it! 3) **Paced** breathing; this means pacing your breathing by slowing it down. The key here is to breathe out more slowly than you breathe in. 4) **Paired** (with Paced breathing) muscle relaxation can also help change your body's chemistry. You can try starting with your feet and moving to your head and then back, or you can do squeeze-and-release if that is more effective for you. The goal is not to "feel more relaxed"; the goal is to learn to notice your body's tension and to cue it to relax when you say the word, "Relax." By helping tension to leave our bodies we become more accepting, less in danger of hanging out in EM.

This skill is very useful when you are stuck in EM and can't get out; when you're in crisis and have a strong urge; or when you're so overwhelmed you can't think how to respond. TIPP works rapidly (within seconds), doesn't require much thought, is easy to use, as effective as medications, as effective as maladaptive behaviors, and some parts of TIPP can be used even when you're in public.

For homework, use DT Worksheets 4, 4a, and 4b, on pages 376 - 378. Try each of these techniques at least once during the week. If you don't have any occasion when you're close to EM, so much the better! Congratulations, and do it anyway. Practice, practice, practice is what helps us have these skills available when we really need them.

Dear DBT skills class,

The skills of the Distress Tolerance module help us to get through the distressing event without hurting ourselves, without hurting anyone else, and without making the situation worse. We've already covered STOP and the TIPP skills. This week we turn our attention to skills that allow us to be distracted from whatever set off the distress. These skills won't help you "feel better" because they won't solve the original problem, but we all deserve a break from feelings of distress. And, by engaging in distracting activities, we may even change how we feel.

The distract skills can be remembered using this acronym: Wise Mind "**ACCEPTS**":

A - Activities: Try activities that you find engaging. The most effective activities are those that are neutral or opposite to unpleasant emotions and crisis behaviors, so probably don't go watching "Beaches" when you're sad. Exercise, cleaning, raking leaves, or watching a funny video are all possibilities.

C - Contributing: Try volunteer work or other altruistic acts. We often feel better when we do things for others. Contributing doesn't have to be a big thing. Smiling at a grocery store clerk or asking a waitperson how they are doing today can have a big impact.

C - Comparisons: Put your situation in context by comparing yourself or your situation in a way that helps you to feel grateful, more confident and capable. The idea here is to get perspective on your problems, not to invalidate yourself or anyone else. This skill is not intended to promote arrogance or thinking you are better than anyone.

E – Change your **Emotions**: Take an action that will produce the opposite emotion (or a less uncomfortable emotion) from the one that is distressing you. First, you have to figure out what your emotion is. Then choose an action that will produce the opposite emotion or at least a less challenging emotion than what you are experiencing. For example, if I'm feeling sad I might go see a funny movie or listen to music that makes me smile. If the opposite emotion seems like too much of a stretch, go for a less afflictive emotion. For example, if you are more comfortable with anger than with sadness, you could go see a documentary on injustices in the world.

P – **Push away** thoughts: Box up your thoughts or use another visualization technique to give yourself a break. It may help to write down the thought(s) and literally put them away for later. Caution: If this skill is your "go to" skill on a daily basis, don't use it! In general, DBT helps us to approach, not avoid. Mostly, this one shouldn't be your first line of defense if you do use it.

T – Substitute other **Thoughts**: Engage in mental exercises such as puzzles, creative acts, counting, or anything that helps to fill up your short-term memory bank. The more cluttered your short-term memory is with Sudoku, multiplication tables, colors, or the names of everyone in your first grade class, the less room there will be for your worry thoughts.

S - Sensations: Distract by running cold or hot water on your hands, snapping a rubber band on your wrist, holding ice, having sex, exercising intensely, or sucking on a lemon.

The homework is DT Worksheets # 5, 5a, <u>or</u> 5b - they are simply three different formats to cover the same skills. They can be found on pages 379-381. In addition, some members recommend an app called Virtual Hope Box. It is DBT-like and has DT skills and meditations. You may find it useful.

Dear DBT skills class,

This week we are practicing self-soothing. The techniques are mostly physical and engage the five senses -- vision, hearing, smell, taste, and touch. The idea behind these is to provide comfort and nurturing to yourself while you have to survive a crisis. You may already be doing some of these; or the concept that you can do things to make yourself feel better and calmer may feel somewhat foreign. However, once you find some that are comfortable for you and practice them, they can be very powerful.

We made magic wands and played with scent, taste, and touch in class. Distress Tolerance Handout #8 (p. 334) gives other examples for each of your five senses, such as...

With **Vision**: Walk in a pretty part of town. Look at the nature around you. Go to a museum with beautiful art. Buy a flower and put it where you can see it. Sit in a garden. Watch the snowflakes decorate the trees during a snowfall. Light a candle and watch the flame. Look at a book with beautiful scenery or beautiful art. Watch a travel movie or video. Look at pictures of people you love.

With **Hearing**: Listen to beautiful or soothing music, or to tapes of the ocean or other sounds of nature. Listen to a baby gurgling or a small animal. Sit by a waterfall. Call a friend to hear their voice. Listen to birds singing.

With **Smell**: Smell breakfast being cooked at home or in a restaurant. Notice all the different smells around you. Walk in a garden or in the woods, maybe just after a rain, and breathe in the smells of nature. Light a scented candle or incense. Bake some bread or a cake, and take in all the smells. Put on scented body lotion (which also engages the sense of touch).

With **Taste**: Have a special treat, and eat it slowly, savoring each bite. Cook a favorite meal - comfort food is comforting for a reason! Drink a soothing drink like herbal tea or hot chocolate. Let the taste run over your tongue and slowly down your throat. Go to a potluck, and eat a little bit of each dish, mindfully tasting each new thing. In the summer, eat fresh fruit from the farmers' market.

With **Touch**: Take a bubble bath. Pet your dog or cat or cuddle a baby. Put on a silk shirt or blouse, and feel its softness and smoothness. Sink into a really comfortable bed. Float or swim in a pool, and feel the water caress your body. Get a massage. Give and get hugs.

As you engage (or try to engage) in self soothing activities, observe thoughts that get in the way, such as "I don't deserve kindness," "This feels odd," "It's not going to work," or "I don't have time." These may be emotional myths getting in the way. It may help to approach self-soothing as something that you will try for a very short time -- such as one minute. You might need to use the skill of Opposite to the Emotion Action to get yourself to practice self-soothing. On the other hand, it's also possible to overuse this skill. When a crisis hits, we have to balance self-soothing with problem-solving. Overuse can lead to more self-destructive behaviors (for example, overeating can itself be self-destructive, and can lead to other problematic behaviors).

For homework, you can choose between DT Worksheets 6, 6a, or 6b: different formats to record the same information. These are on pages 382-384. Or you can use DT Worksheet 6c on page 385, which is a way to practice a body scan meditation. A body scan can also be self-soothing, as we focus on the present moment and body sensations; we become more in tune with Body Mind than Emotion Mind.

Dear DBT skills class,

This week we learned about the **IMPROVE** skill. IMPROVE stands for a set of strategies that can make it easier for you to survive a distressing situation without making it worse, because they improve the quality of the present moment. IMPROVE the moment skills replace immediate, unpleasant, events with more pleasant ones.

I(magery): With imagery, you create a situation different from the one that is causing you distress. Imagery can be very useful for flashbacks, for example, because you can use it to create a safe room or safe haven that you go to in your mind during or after flashbacks. Imagery can also increase confidence if you imagine yourself coping well - athletes do this by repeatedly imagining their future performances in great detail. The idea here is either to imagine yourself coping skillfully with whatever is distressing you or to imagine very relaxing scenes, safe havens, or a calming and beautiful fantasy world. Imagery must be practiced when there is not a crisis in order for it to be effective during crisis situations.

M(eaning): Find or create some purpose, meaning, or value in your pain. Making meaning changes your appraisal of the situation - as one former group member once said, it is like putting a new frame around a picture. It is "making lemonade out of lemons." You do not have to believe that <u>everything</u> happens for a reason, but you create a reason for <u>this</u> pain.

P(rayer): This skill decreases distress by increasing your acceptance. You do not have to be religious for prayer to work: you can pray to God or to a higher being or to your own Wise Mind.

R(elaxing actions): this changes your body's response to a crisis and works with the mind-body connection. If you can relax your body, this feeds back to your mind and stops the <u>increase</u> in pain. When you're relaxed, it's easier to resist the urge to behave in a problematic way, and to think of creative solutions. Choose the activity that is most relaxing for you: progressive muscle relaxation, relaxation tapes, exercising hard, deep breathing, massage, and hot baths are all examples. This must be practiced regularly for it to be useful during a crisis.

O(ne thing in the moment): This is essentially the same skill that you already know from Core Mindfulness: being one-mindful. The secret to this skill is remembering that you only have to survive this pain, just for this moment. Don't think about past crises, and don't wonder when this one will end or what disaster is coming next. Just focus on this one moment; that's all you have to get through.

(Mini-)V(acation): Everyone needs a vacation from time to time. The trick is to make it a mini-vacation - no longer than a day, and usually about 30 minutes. Take a time out to regroup and catch your breath. If you have responsibilities, first get someone to take them over, before you take your mini-vacation. Then pull the covers over your head, make a blanket fort, or curl up with a trashy novel and let it all go for a while.

E(encourage yourself): This is cheerleading yourself. Just as you would to a friend, say positive and encouraging things, not put-downs and criticisms. When you have to do something really hard, when it seems as if the crisis will never end, when the situation seems hopeless, put on those pom-poms and become a cheerleader.

Your homework is DT Worksheets 7, 7a, and 7b, on pages 386-388. Please remember that these skills must be practiced often to build up your coping muscles.

Dear DBT Skills Class,

This week we continued in the Distress Tolerance module, with the first two of the reality acceptance skills (there are five in all). The goals of these skills are to reduce your suffering and increase your sense of freedom by helping you to come to terms with the facts of your life. This is particularly useful when the life you're living is not the one you want. We will return to Radical Acceptance; this week we studied Distress Tolerance Handouts #12, Turning the Mind, and #13, Willingness (pp. 345-346). This week's skills are important because in order to accept a reality that we don't like, we usually have to make the effort more than once. We sometimes have to keep accepting reality over and over and over – for a long time.

When we think about the skill of **Turning the Mind**, we can think about standing at a fork in the road. Instead of turning your mind toward the road of rejection, complaining, stubborn willfulness, or even refusing to take either fork, when we turn the mind we turn toward the road of acceptance. By turning your mind, you may not yet have radically accepted – but you're on the way. You can turn your mind to <u>try to</u> accept. Maybe you haven't gotten there yet, but at least you aren't rejecting – that's progress!

So how do we do it? The good news is that you already have these skills. First, use the Observe skill to notice that you're not accepting. Hints that you're not on the acceptance road include irritation, anger, bitterness, rumination, or any of the ways you avoid. Maybe your physical condition is giving you hints: shoulders up around your ears, fists clenched. You may have to use the skill of Opposite to the Emotion Action to take the next step, which is to make a commitment to yourself to turn away from rejection and to turn your mind toward acceptance. You can make a commitment to acknowledge the facts - that's not acceptance, but it's a step on the acceptance road. Then – do this again, over and over and over. We never turn the mind just once; we have to keep doing it. This is especially true if reality is painful.

We also looked at DT Handout #13, on **Willingness**. This skill is defined as, "readiness to enter and participate fully in life and living." This is hard to do when you don't like what life is handing you. Willingness is the opposite of willfulness. Willfulness is refusal to tolerate the moment, refusing to make needed changes, holding a grudge, saying, "Yes, but….", being passive, giving up. It's also trying to control, to fix every situation. This skill asks us to find a <u>willing</u> response in each situation. That means doing just what is needed in that particular situation. It is wholeheartedly accepting and responding to what is. Willingness means responding from Wise Mind. If this is really difficult for you, it may help to ask yourself, "What's the threat, here? What's the catastrophe I'm afraid of if I try a willing response?"

Acceptance of reality starts with observing our willfulness and turning the mind even a little bit away from willfulness and toward acceptance and willingness.

The homework is DT Worksheet #10, on page 396. Remember that Turning the Mind doesn't have to mean that you take a giant step; you can turn the mind, like turning your head, just a few degrees. Even a small turning will make some difference, if you are willing.

Dear DBT skills class,

Our emotions are partly controlled by our bodies and our facial expressions, so we can accept reality by practicing Half-smiling and Willing Hands. These are found on DT Handout #14, page 347, with suggested practice exercises on pages 348-349.

When you practice **Half-Smile**, relax your face from the top of the head to the chin and jaw. Then, turn up the corners of your lips slightly. When you have a serene, accepting face you will feel more serene and accepting.

Willing Hands recognizes that your hands communicate to your brain just as your face does, so you can turn your mind from angry willfulness to willingness by having willing hands. This can be done at any time: unclench your hands, turn your palms upward, and relax your fingers.

The skill of **Mindfulness of Current Thoughts** (DT Handouts #15 and 15a, pp. 350-352) is another reality acceptance skill because we are allowing our mind to have thoughts; we let them come into or drift out of our minds, noticing the thoughts but not changing them. When we notice our thoughts as if they are boats drifting by on the river, we are stepping back from the thoughts. It's also important to remember that thoughts are not facts: thoughts are sensations of the brain, that come and go. Usually, when we have a worry thought, we grab hold of it, we react immediately, we <u>do something</u>. This skill asks you to do exactly the opposite: <u>do nothing</u> other than notice that you're having the thought.

The goal of the skill of Mindfulness of Current Thoughts is not an empty mind. We're not trying to block or suppress thoughts. We're not trying to change the thoughts from unpleasant ones to pleasant ones. We're changing our relationship to our thoughts, not changing the thoughts themselves.

For homework, please complete DT Worksheet # 11 or 11a (page 397 or 398) and DT Worksheet 12 or 12a (page 399 or 400). Play around with more than one of the suggestions given in DT Handouts 14a and 15a. Try Half-smile while thinking of someone you dislike. Try Mindfulness of Current Thoughts by putting the thoughts on a conveyor belt, or a balloon, or a cloud. We look forward to hearing your experiences with these skills

Dear DBT skills class,

Now that you have a foundation in acceptance (turning the mind, willingness, half-smile and willing hands, mindfulness of current thoughts), we finished up our study of acceptance skills to tolerate distress by learning what some people think is the hardest one of all: Radical Acceptance. We looked at DT Handouts 10, 11, 11a, and 11b (pages 341-344).

Radical Acceptance is complete and total openness to the facts as they are, without pitching a fit or responding to the facts ineffectively with willfulness. It is accepting something all the way, mind and body. We are only accepting facts. When we refuse to accept the facts we can feel despair, bitterness, resentment, even shame and guilt. We can also feel this way when we accept something other than facts, such as myths or fears.

We only have to accept facts about the past and the present, and reasonable probabilities about the future. Everyone's future has limitations, and we must radically accept this, as well. We can be limited by the environment, by our biology, by our past behavior. But fears about the future don't have to be accepted as known probabilities. Thoughts about the future are not facts about the future.

Why should we accept reality? First, rejecting it or denying it doesn't change it. And changing reality first requires that we accept it. Besides, suffering is the result of pain plus our non-acceptance of that pain. It takes a boatload of DT skills to stop our target behaviors (self-injury, stealing, using drugs and alcohol, angry outbursts), but the only way out of hell is to radically accept the misery we are going to feel for a while, not using the old target behaviors.

There are three types of situations where RA is really useful: 1) life has handed you a major trauma, pain, or difficulty; 2) you are in distress but not in a crisis; or 3) problem-solving isn't working. In the latter case, you may need to evaluate whether you're trying to solve the right problem - whether you have actually accepted all the facts of reality.

Radical Acceptance is not approval. It is not compassion or love. It is not passivity, giving up, or giving in. It's not opposed to change - in fact, acceptance is essential in order to bring about change.

A list of the factors that interfere with RA is found on DT Handout #11a, page 343. Handout #11b (p. 344) tells you how to practice RA, step by step. This accompanies the homework, which is DT Worksheet #9 and 9a on pages 394 and 395. We strongly recommend that you use Worksheet #9 to get some solid practice in on this challenging (but essential for progress) skill.

DBT Reminder: Alternate Rebellion and Adaptive Denial

Dear DBT Skills class,

This week we learned how to apply the Distress Tolerance (crisis survival) skills to the crisis of addiction. Think you don't have any addictive behaviors? You might be surprised. DT Handout #16a, on page 356, lists many, many things we can become addicted to. The definition of addiction is: in spite of negative consequences, and in spite of having tried to quit, <u>you can't stop</u>. Alcohol and drugs are obvious ones, but what about checking your phone? shopping? driving too fast? eating? dieting? lying? stealing? caffeine? sugar? TV? gossiping? The list is rather long.

Any time your brain experiences reward, there's the risk of addiction. Initially the pleasure you experience is the positive reinforcer (the reward, the benefit, the goody), but over time you develop a need to eliminate your craving – that's the reward. Some addictions are physical; we can put alcohol, drugs, caffeine, nicotine, and other substances in this category. But if the addictive behavior is a way for you to express your rebellion against authority, or rules, or conformity, then DT Handout #21 (page 363) offers the skills of Alternate Rebellion and Adaptive Denial.

With **Alternate Rebellion**, we replace destructive rebellious behaviors with ones that allow you to keep moving toward your life-worth-living goals. Tattoos can be an example of Alternate Rebellion. There is a list in the handout of some others.

The skill of **Adaptive Denial** gives you permission, for once, to use denial. So, when the urge to practice your addictive behavior grabs you, deny it. Deny that you want the substance; deny that you want to practice the behavior. "Nope, not me! I don't have any more cravings, and boy is my life better!" You tell yourself that you don't crave what you think you're craving. Or you can put off the addictive behavior for just 5 minutes. "I can have a cigarette in five minutes, but not now." Keep doing this (it's a version of Urge Surfing). Just don't replace one addictive behavior with another.

If you have - or think you have - any addictions, please take them to your individual therapist and try applying these skills to them.

The homework is Distress Tolerance Worksheet #18, on page 410. We look forward to hearing your adventures. In addition, since next week will be the review of the entire Distress Tolerance module, please bring any questions or arguments you have for us to include.

Dear DBT skills class,
   This week we reviewed the Distress Tolerance module.

   When you find yourself in a distressing situation that is beyond your control, experiment with your repertoire of skills. Use **ACCEPTS** to distract yourself; use the **self-soothe** skills for self-care and nurturing; and change your perception of your body's reaction to a situation when you **IMPROVE** the moment. As needed, pull in Reason Mind and use your **Pros & Cons** to reinforce the value of tolerating distress (rather than rejecting it, fighting it, or giving in to responses that may be very familiar and easier in the moment but that make things worse).

   Continue to turn your mind toward a **radical acceptance** of difficult things that just are. The more willing we are to accept things that we cannot change, the less difficult and overwhelming they will feel. Remember, acceptance is not the same as approving of a situation. It is not resignation, either. It is more an acknowledgement that there are things beyond our control and that we can make the choice to accept this. There is a relief that comes with this kind of acceptance. It can end our fighting battles that we cannot win. It also helps reduce feelings of distress and move us toward more effective problem solving. Often, we have to remind ourselves over and over to be willing to move in this direction.

During this module, we listed several characteristics of the DT skills:
   1. They may not make you feel better (but they won't make you feel worse)
   2. They will not solve the problem (but they won't make it worse)
   3. They will move you toward Reason Mind
   4. Be like a Girl Scout: be prepared! Have your self-soothe kit packed and handy by; know which Activity tends to work best to distract you; have a favorite Relaxation you like. Practice, practice, practice, so the skills are at your fingertips when you eventually need them.
   5. Just because you are using all your skills doesn't mean you won't occasionally fall apart. But when you do, you won't fall apart for as long, or as hard, or in as self-damaging ways as you did in the past.

   For homework, please complete DT Worksheet #1 on page 369 (or 1a or 1b, as you prefer). Continue to review and use your DT skills. Please try your "old favorites" as well as some of the skills you don't usually use. Think about how you can incorporate these skills into your daily life (which tends to present us with plenty of distressing situations!).

Appendices

The Seven Steps of Participating

Wake up
Get up
Show up
Act as if you care
Do it half-heartedly
Do it whole-heartedly
Do it with FLOW

From: Meggan Moorhead, EdD with Mareah Steketee, PhD. Used with permission (personal communication, April 8, 2020).

INTERPERSONAL EFFECTIVENESS HANDOUT 5

Cheerleading Statements
for Interpersonal Effectiveness

1. It is OK to want or need something from someone else.

2. I have a choice to ask someone for what I want or need.

3. I can stand it if I don't get what I want or need.

4. The fact that someone says no to my request doesn't mean I should not have asked in the first place.

5. If I didn't get my objectives, that doesn't mean I didn't go about it in a skillful way.

6. Standing up for myself over "small" things can be just as important as "big" things are to others.

7. I can insist on my rights and still be a good person.

8. I sometimes have a right to assert myself, even though I may inconvenience others.

9. The fact that other people might not be assertive doesn't mean that I shouldn't be.

10. I can understand and validate another person, and still ask for what I want.

11. There is no law that says other people's opinions are more valid than mine.

12. I may want to please people I care about, but I don't have to please them all the time.

13. Giving, giving, giving is not the be-all of life. I am an important person in this world, too.

14. If I refuse to do a favor for people, that doesn't mean I don't like them. They will probably understand that, too.

15. I am under no obligation to say yes to people simply because they ask a favor of me.

16. The fact that I say no to someone does not make me a selfish person.

17. If I say no to people and they get angry, that does not mean that I should have said yes.

18. I can still feel good about myself, even though someone else is annoyed with me.

OTHERS: ____

____

____

____

119

From: Marsha Linehan, <u>Skills Training Manual for Treating Borderline Personality Disorder</u>, 1993, p. 119. Reprinted with permission of Guilford Press.

INTERPERSONAL EFFECTIVENESS HANDOUT 7

Suggestions for Interpersonal Effectiveness Practice

Interpersonal skills can only be learned if they are PRACTICED, PRACTICED, PRACTICED. To do this, you must be alert to every practice opportunity. If no situations arise naturally, then you may need to go out of your way to find or create opportunities to practice. Some of the following situations are examples of what you can create for practice. Others are situations that may arise in your day-to-day life.

1. Go to a library and ask the librarian for assistance in finding a book. (Variation: ask salesperson to help you find something.)
2. While talking with someone, change the subject.
3. Invite a friend to dinner (at your house or at a restaurant).
4. Call an insurance company and ask about its rates.
5. Take old books to a used-book store and find out what they are worth. Leave after you have your information.
6. Pay for a newspaper, pack of gum, or anything else costing less than $.50 with a $5.00 bill.
7. In a drug store or candy store, ask for change for a $1.00 bill without buying anything.
8. Go to a luncheonette or lunch counter during a slack time and ask for a glass of water, drink it, say "Thank you," and walk out again.
9. Go into a restaurant and ask to use the restroom; leave without eating anything.
10. Phone the department of sanitation, ask to speak to the commissioner (or as highly placed an official as you can reach), and complain about the garbage collection in your neighborhood. (Variations on this theme are numerous—e.g., complaining about telephone service, newspaper delivery, taxi service, bus service, bad TV program, etc.)
11. Go to a full-service gas station and ask the attendant to check the water in your radiator (or air in your tires); leave without buying gas.
12. Get on a bus (or wait for a bus) and ask other passengers for change. (Variations on this theme are numerous - asking someone for change for a newspaper, parking meter, etc.)
13. Call and make an appointment to have your hair cut. Call back later and cancel the appointment. (Variations: Make and cancel dinner reservations; make and cancel airline reservations.)
14. Ask the pharmacist for information on an over-the-counter drug.
15. Ask for special "fixings" on a sandwich bought at McDonald's, Burger King, or another fast-food restaurant. A variation of this is to ask for a substitution on the menu when ordering a meal.
16. Ask a salesperson in a store to help you find something.
17. Ask the manager in the supermarket to order something that you would like to buy but the store doesn't now carry.

(cont.)

From *Skills Training Manual for Treating Borderline Disorder* by Marsha Linehan. © 1993 The Guilford Press.

123

From: Marsha Linehan, <u>Skills Training Manual for Treating Borderline Personality Disorder</u>, 1993, pp. 123-124. Reprinted with permission of Guilford Press.

18. Ask a clerk in the grocery store whether they have any fresher lettuce (or other fruit or vegetable) in the back of the store. (Variation: Ask the clerk to check whether an item you want is in the back if you don't find it on the shelf.)

19. Go to a deli counter and ask for 2 ounces of meat or cheese. Leave without buying anything else.

20. Go into a department store or gift store and ask the salesperson for help in choosing an item or a gift. (Variation: Ask salesperson for an opinion on outfit you are considering buying.)

21. Call and ask for information about jobs listed in the classified section of the newspaper. (Variations on this theme are numerous: Call about things being sold in the classified ads; call universities and ask for information about classes; etc.)

22. Ask coworkers or classmates to do a favor for you (e.g., fix you a cup of coffee while they are fixing their own, give you an opinion on some aspect of your work, etc.).

23. Ask someone for a ride.

24. Disagree with someone's opinion.

25. Express disagreement with a parent, spouse, partner, or close friend regarding specific topics (scheduling priorities, sexual practices, time spent together, etc.).

26. Express disagreement over social arrangements as planned by a parent, spouse, partner, or close friend.

27. Request parent, spouse, partner, or children to accept more responsibility in some specific area.

28. Ask a friend for help in fixing something.

29. Ask a person making too much noise to be a bit quieter (person talking in a movie, neighbor playing loud music, etc.).

30. Ask your therapist or counselor for a favor.

31. Ask for help in moving furniture.

32. Ask your landlord to fix leaky roof, faucet, broken appliances, creaky door, etc.

33. Go see a dentist or physician and tell him or her clearly what the problem is.

34. Order a nonalcoholic beverage in a bar or cocktail lounge.

35. Ask to be excused from class or ask to leave early.

36. Ask a person to stop doing something that bothers you.

37. Ask skills training leader (who is going overtime) to end the session because time is up.

38. Ask a teacher for time to speak to him or her and make a complaint or give a compliment about the class.

Other: ____

____

____

From: Marsha Linehan, <u>Skills Training Manual for Treating Borderline Personality Disorder</u>, 1993, pp. 123-124. Reprinted with permission of Guilford Press.

42 Ways to Say 'No'
(or buy time until you can)

A lot of us have difficulty saying "No". This list, offered with compassion and a little humor, will help you get comfortable with turning people down, refusing to answer nosy or offensive questions, asking people to stop doing something you don't like, and telling others you disagree with them.

As you develop your "No" muscles, see if you can shift from saying, "I can't" to forthrightly saying, "I won't." Also try exchanging, "I don't want you to..." for, "Don't...". You will feel vastly more empowered -- and have more time for yourself and the people you really care about when you do.

When Someone Asks You To Do Something For Them or With Them

1. The enthusiastic (polite/helpful/etc.) part of me would like to say yes, but the rest of me is overcommitted (more realistic/unwilling/etc.).
2. I don't know. I'll have to think that over.
3. I wish I could help you out, but I'm overextended/overcommitted right now.
4. I'm going to pass. I'm really trying to slow down my pace these days.
5. That's something I'll have to think about.
6. I don't have my calendar with me, but I can call and let you know tomorrow.
7. Sorry, I'm already booked.
8. No, I can't make it after all. But it was nice of you to ask.
9. I'll think it over.
10. Thanks, but I'm way too tired.
11. No, that's not really my thing.
12. Don't hold your breath!
13. I have an appointment that day/night. (And you don't have to say what it is!)
14. That's not for me, thanks.
15. Oh, that sounds interesting. Let me think about it and get back to you.
16. I'm not sure if I'm free that day/night. Let me check and call you tomorrow.
17. Sorry, but my schedule is too full right now.

18. The part that wants to make you happy wants to say yes, but the rest of me won the vote. I'll pass.
19. Thanks, but I don't think I will.
20. That's not really something I enjoy.
21. That doesn't work for me.
22. That doesn't fit for me.
23. When you want to have some fun saying no, try one of these: Not in this lifetime! Forget it! Dream on! No way, Jose! You must be kidding! Not in a million years! Are you out of your mind?

When Someone Does, Asks, or Says or Asks Something Invasive

24. I'm not comfortable with that.
25. I'd like to ask you not to ___________________________________.
26. I'd like you to stop ___________________________________.
27. Please stop doing that. I don't like it.
28. I'm uncomfortable right now with what you're saying/doing.
29. That's not something I talk about except with family.
30. Let's talk about something else.
31. I want to keep that to myself.
32. That's my business.
33. I'm surprised you think you have a right to that information.
34. I don't feel like talking about it.
35. And you are asking me this because... ?? (Try saying this with a look of utter disbelief.)
36. Sorry, that's not something I talk about.
37. I never answer questions like that.

When Someone Says Something You Disagree With

38. I see it differently than you do.
39. We certainly don't agree about that.
40. I have a different point of view.
41. My experience of ___________________________ is somewhat different.
42. I hear what you are saying, but I don't agree with it.

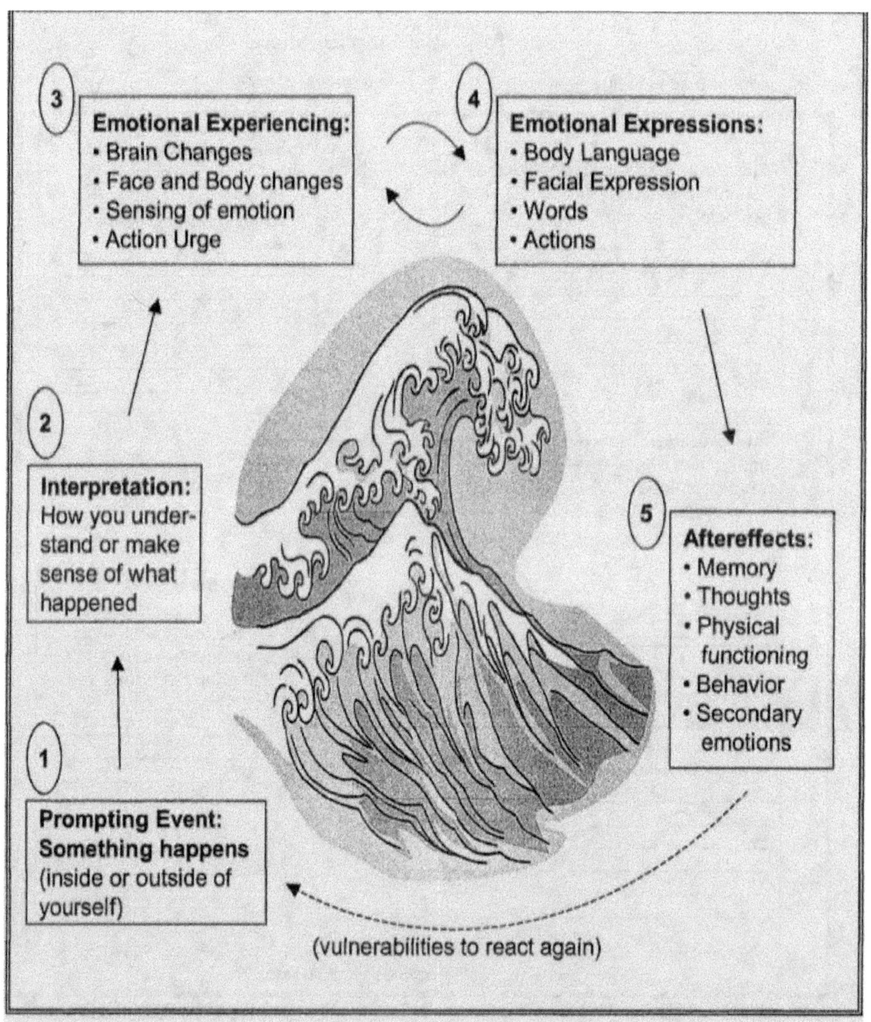

From: Seth Axelrod, PhD, adapted from Marsha Linehan's <u>Skills Training Manual for Treating Borderline Personality Disorder</u> (1993). Used with permission (personal communication, February 19, 2020)

Opposite-to-the-Emotion Action for Shame and Guilt

<u>Ask:</u> Will I be rejected from a group I care about if my behavior or personal characteristics become public knowledge?

		NO	YES
<u>Ask</u>: Does my behavior violate my own Wise Mind values?	**NO**	A. Unjustified (both)	C. Justified shame (I don't disapprove but others will reject me)
	YES	B. Justified guilt (I disapprove but others won't reject me)	D. Justified (both)

OTEA works best when:
- Knowing the facts doesn't help (she didn't mean to hurt you but you're still angry)

- The emotion, its intensity, or its duration are unjustified

- The emotion, its intensity, or its duration isn't effective for meeting your goals (a car wreck creates a traffic jam when you're in a hurry. Anger is justified but ineffective – it won't help you get there any faster)

- When you're avoiding what needs to be done.

See handout 10 for the steps of OTEA

Adapted from Marsha Linehan's <u>Skills Training Manual for Treating Borderline Personality Disorder</u> (1993), Guilford Press.

Check your VITALS: How to do what you do not feel like doing!

V **Validate** the 10,000 pound cloak of, "I can't," "It's too scary," "I don't want to," or, "It won't be good enough." What is the sentence that holds you back? What part of it might be true? Where is the nugget of wisdom? Come into a friendly relationship with   yourself.
Behavioral Skill of Validation

I **Imagine** yourself as vividly as possible doing the behavior in the way you would like to do it, peacefully and productively, or confidently and lightly. How clearly can you see?
Behavioral Skill of Imaginal Practice

T **Take small steps**. Ask yourself, "What is the tiniest step I could take toward this activity, assignment, or challenge?" Breaking a complex behavior down is a powerful step towards finding willingness.   *Behavioral Skill of Successive Approximations*

A **Applaud** Find and use positive phrases in your mind or physical gestures that give you encouragement or appreciation such as "I did it", "You go", " I can do this", fist in the air, hand on your heart, or clapping.
Behavioral Skill of Positive Reinforcement

L **Lighten the Load** Let yourself recall what suffering you can lessen by taking this step. If I do X I won't have to experience Y.
Behavioral Skill of Negative Reinforcement

S **Sweeten the Pot** Find objects or activities that you can give yourself once you have begun (coffee, music) or when you are done (call or text a friend, sit in the sun, watch Netflix, read a book, take a nap, take a walk). What can you give yourself that will increase the likelihood you will do it? This is the most powerful reinforcer of all.
Behavioral Skill of Positive Reinforcement

Building Mastery

A google search for the phrase "building mastery" pulls up thousands of sites about random things people can build mastery in, which include:

- Guitar playing
- Learning other musical instruments
- Reading
- Spelling
- Arithmetic
- Managing your money better
- Cooking
- Building things
- Using an axe properly for medieval jousting tournaments
- Sewing
- Bead work
- Advertising campaigns
- Using a search engine
- Designing a website
- Tae kwan do
- Teaching
- Riding a horse
- Controlling your dog
- Making your marriage work
- Being a more effective parent
- Communicating clearly and assertively
- Running/developing a company/ business
- Diagnosing and treating critically ill patients
- Persuasive speech
- A foreign language
- Craft work
- Talking to people – joining groups
- Drawing comic books
- Origami

So what do you wish to master – what new skills would you like to learn/practice that will make you feel more competent/ confident / good about yourself?

Set yourself some goals and quietly work away at them, discuss this with your individual therapist – strive to be building mastery every day in some area of your life.

From: C. Young, 2008

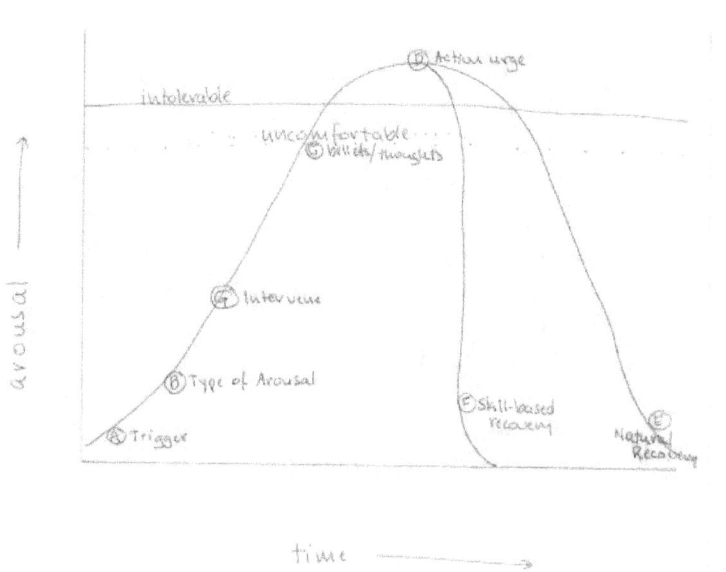

From: Chuck Holton, LCSW, and Mareah Steketee, PhD. Used with permission (personal communication, April 2, 2020).

The Wave of Over-Arousal
    A. Trigger
        a. When am I vulnerable to over-arousal?
        b. What kinds of things set me off?
        c. Any specific examples recently?
    B. Type of Arousal
        a. Fear/panic
        b. Rage/anger
        c. Craving/Addiction
        d. Loss/sadness
        e. Shame/guilt
        f. Mania
    C. Beliefs/Thoughts
        a. Will it ever end unless I act on the urge?
        b. I have to….
        c. I have no choice…
        d. It's the only way to feel better
        e. Speculation about the future
    D. Action urge
        a. Yelling
        b. Drinking
        c. Withdrawing
        d. Self-harm
        e. Compulsion
        f. Overworking
        g. Overspending
        h. Ruminating
        i. Impulsive behavior
    E. Natural Recovery
        a. How long does it take?
        b. How do I know it is better?
    F. Skill-based recovery (e.g., Emotion Regulation, Distress Tolerance)
        a. What skills do you already use that help?
        b. What new skills can you practice?
    G. Intervention before over-arousal (e.g., Emotion Regulation)
        a. What skills do you already use that help?
        b. What new skills can you practice?

From: Chuck Holton, LCSW, and Mareah Steketee, PhD. Used with permission (personal communication, April 2, 2020)

 DBT *Holiday Antidotes*

DBT Top Ten Holiday Antidotes

10. The holidays can be rough going, so let's begin by planning some small, doable, positive and pleasurable experiences. *Do them.* Mindfully notice the positives in your life. Each day note something for which you genuinely feel gratitude. Find one meaningful thing to do today.

9. All things in moderation. Use the PLEASE skills to lessen your emotional vulnerability—which only get more intense when negative Emotion Mind meets alcohol, non-mindful eating (under-control and over-control) and other old, unwise attempts to deal with stress.

8. The holidays are a great time to use the "contributing" skill to distract and interrupt increasing depression or anxiety by visiting or helping those in need, perhaps as close as a next-door neighbor.

7. Have access to music, a symbolic object, a photo, a pleasant smell, a comforting taste or touch. Also some quiet time with a hot bath, a good book, a loving animal, a kind human, or your compassionate, wise mind can provide some self-soothing when the holidays get tense.

6. Observe that emotions come and emotions go. The holidays often amplify the intensity of negative emotions. When you find your sadness, anger or fear rising and approaching the "red zone," try taking a walk to get a working distance from the situation, remember your goals, and be sure to give yourself some validation. If possible, grab a trusted loved one to go with you.

5. Holidays are also prime viewing time to observe our negative thoughts, such as catastrophizing, all-or-nothing, and "should" thoughts. Getting hooked by our "twisted thinking" leads to unneeded suffering. Let's use this time as an opportunity to practice "letting go" or "not buying" negative thinking or ruminating on past grievances. Instead, let's participate in the present moment as it is.

4. Steer clear of holiday regrets by listening to wise mind and effectively responding to difficult family members. What does my wise mind say now? Listen. Cultivate a "mindful gap" in a tense, reactive situation. Walk away knowing you have successfully "surfed the urge" and sidestepped a potential round of conflict. Apply DEAR with GIVE or FAST when you can.

3. Communicate! Invite your curiosity to the conversation. Clarify your priorities in the interaction: making progress on an objective or task, maintaining a relationship, or standing up for yourself. Express or ask for what you need. Say "no" when you need to. Say "yes" when you choose.

2. Observe the judgmental thoughts. Re-describe in a non-judgmental way. What would you say to a close friend in the same situation? Help yourself to accept this moment as it is and to accept yourself as you are. Some wisdom with a good dose of compassion.

And the #1 Antidote... Mindfully Breathe 3x... mindfully... ahh... Repeat, as needed.

From: John Mader, LCSW, adapted from Marsha Linehan's <u>Skills Training Manual for Borderline Personality Disorder</u> (2015). Used with permission (personal communication, February 20, 2020).

Holiday Antidotes Worksheet

Which skills have been useful during past holidays?

1.

2.

3.

Which of the above skills would be useful to do this holiday season?

Which of the other skills or holiday antidotes do you want to use this year?

1.

2.

3.

And what will help you to willingly use these skills, especially when you are becoming distressed and could be heading into the Red Zone?

From: John Mader, LCSW, adapted from Marsha Linehan's <u>Skills Training Manual for Borderline Personality Disorder</u> (2015). Used with permission (personal communication, February 20, 2020).